Enoch Pond

The Seals Opened

The Apocalypse Explained

Enoch Pond

The Seals Opened
The Apocalypse Explained

ISBN/EAN: 9783337414696

Printed in Europe, USA, Canada, Australia, Japan

Cover: Foto ©Lupo / pixelio.de

More available books at **www.hansebooks.com**

THE

SEALS OPENED;

OR, THE

APOCALYPSE EXPLAINED.

BY

ENOCH POND, D.D.,

PROFESSOR IN THE THEOLOGICAL SEMINARY, BANGOR.

PORTLAND:

HOYT, FOGG, AND BREED.

MDCCCLXXI.

PREFACE.

I HAVE long wished to come to a clear and right understanding of the Apocalypse. It has been a subject of thought and inquiry with me almost from childhood. Years ago, I flattered myself that I might interpret the first five chapters and the last three; but all between the sixth chapter and the twentieth seemed dark and mysterious. In the midst of unexplained visions and symbols I was confounded, and could see nothing clearly; and it seemed strange to me, that a book so sublime and beautiful, so well attested as a revelation from God, and in regard to which a special blessing has been pronounced upon him who reads and understands it, should have been left in so much darkness.

When the Jesuit and German method of interpreting the book had been published in America, and especially after it had been endorsed substantially by Professor Moses Stuart, I gave the subject a new and earnest attention. But for reasons which will appear in the following pages, I could not adopt the theory proposed. It seemed to me to be based upon a false assumption as to the date of the Apocalypse, and instead of shedding light upon the previous darkness, it the rather increased it.

One thing which deterred me, and I presume has deterred others, from a careful study of the Apocalypse, was a supposed diversity of opinion among standard English and American commentators in regard to it. We were told that our best expositors differed endlessly respecting it, that no two of them were agreed, and that it was impossible to obtain satisfaction, or to find the truth. But, on examination, I am satisfied that this diversity has been much exaggerated. Erratic minds, to be sure, have wandered variously; but among better men, if there has not been an *entire*, there has yet been a *substantial* agreement. The two writers who, beyond others, have served to direct public opinion on the subject in America and in England, are Mr Lowman[1] and Bishop Newton. Following them, on substantially the same plan of interpretation, are Doddrige, Scott, Andrew Fuller, and (better than all), the lamented Albert Barnes. Though not adopting the interpretations of the latter on all points, I feel bound to say, that I have been more assisted by the study of his Notes than by any other author.

The view which he takes, and which I have been

[1] More than fifty years ago, Dr Emmons said to me: 'Lowman's "Paraphrase and Notes on the Revelation" is the best book on the subject that has ever been written.'

led to take, is not new. Avoiding the theories of
Rationalists and Roman Catholics on the one hand,
and of the Adventists on the other, the plan of interpretation which we have pursued is the same
which has been held by the great body of evange-
lical ministers and Christians in America and in
England for the last hundred years. And, in my
opinion, the time has come, when this view should
be more openly and formally adopted in our Churches
than it ever has been. Why should not the Apocalypse be studied in our Sabbath schools and Bible
classes, as well as the other books of the New Testament? It seems to me that public opinion has become sufficiently settled in regard to the explanation of it, to admit of its being made a formal study;
and helps for the understanding of it can be easily
furnished.

A single consideration is sufficient to show that
the symbols of the Apocalypse are not of so difficult
interpretation as some have supposed, and that the
right interpretation has been adopted. The apostle
John, under the inspiration of the Holy Ghost, published, some eighteen hundred years ago, a *prophetic
delineation* of the Decline and Fall of the Roman empire. In the last century, Edward Gibbon published
a *learned history* of its Decline and Fall, and surely no
one will impute to Gibbon a design of recording the
fulfilment of the Apocalypse. And yet Mr Barnes

tells us: ' To my surprise, I found in Gibbon a recorded series of events, which seemed to me to
correspond, to a great extent, with the series of
symbols found in the Apocalypse.'[1]   In other places,
Mr Barnes speaks of Gibbon's history as his principal help in explaining the Seals and the Trumpets.
To this statement I desire to add my own attesta-
tion; I have carefully read Mr Gibbon's history,
having the symbols of the Apocalypse particularly
in view, and I can truly say, that the many obvious
coincidences surprised me.

It has been objected to the Apocalypse—more
especially to the prophetic parts of it—that it is
without plan or method.   But this is not true.   It
has a method which—excepting here and there an
episode—and its triumphant songs—is strictly
pursued.

The prophetical part of the Apocalypse—that
relating to ' the things which shall be hereafter'—
is divided into two parts.

The first train of predictions terminates at the
Millennium. The Seven Seals, including the Trumpets, run on to this stage; for when the seventh angel
sounded, there were great voices in heaven, saying,
' The kingdoms of this world have become the kingdoms of our Lord, and of His Christ, and He shall
reign for ever and ever.'   But, as the latter part of

---

[1] See Albert Barnes' Preface.

this long period is but dimly indicated by the Seals and Trumpets, it is further exhibited in successive symbols and visions, in order to make the view more complete. These commence — perhaps not all at once — with the rise of the Papal power, and extend onward to the Millennium through the 1260 years. The first two of these symbols are the treading of the holy city, the Church, under foot by the Gentiles, for forty and two months, and the prophesying of the two witnesses in sackcloth for the same period (Rev. xi. 2, 3). The third is that of the woman fleeing into the wilderness, to be nourished and protected there for the same period (Rev. xii.) And the fourth is that of the two beasts which were to continue their ravages for the same time (Rev. xiii. 5). These all spread over the same period, and terminate in the great conflict immediately preceding the Millennium.

And, as though these had not depicted events with sufficient fulness and clearness, they are supplemented by several other symbols and visions. There is the vision of the great harlot riding on the Roman beast, and of the seven angels pouring out their vials — the seven *last plagues;* of the terrific fall of the mystical Babylon; and of the closing victory of the Son of God (Rev. xvi.–xix.)

The second train of apocalyptic predictions includes the Millennium; the defection following it;

the overthrow of Gog and Magog, together with all God's enemies; the resurrection and general judgment; the final state of the wicked in the lake of fire; and the endless glories of the Church in heaven.

It will be seen that here is plan and method. The more complicated part of it is the 1260 years preceding the Millennium, where several visions are recorded, not following each other chronologically, but spreading over the same period, for the purpose of a more full delineation. But all this will be more fully explained as we pass along.

It has been no part of my object to write a critical commentary on the Apocalypse, or a learned, elaborate exposition of it. I have designed rather to enlarge and open the book, to show briefly the import and application of its symbols; to point out its fulfilment in the past history of the Church and of her enemies; and, as an encouragement to effort, to present her glorious future. My design, in short, has been so to present this last book of the Bible, that it may be read and understood by Christians generally, feeling sure that they will find it, like all other Scripture, to be 'profitable for doctrine, for reproof, for correction, for instruction in righteousness.'

THEOLOGICAL SEMINARY, BANGOR, ME.,
May 6, 1871.

CONTENTS.

———◆———

CHAPTER I.

Page

The Apocalypse; When Written, and by Whom? . . 1

CHAPTER II.

Review of Professor Stuart on the Apocalypse : with Occasional References to the Commentary of Professor
Cowles, ... 17

CHAPTER III.

The First Three Chapters Considered. Revelation, chaps.
i., ii., iii., ... 30

CHAPTER IV.

Introduction to the Prophetical Portion. Revelation, chaps.
iv., v., ... 37

CHAPTER V.

The Opening of the Seals. Revelation, chap. vi., . . 52

CHAPTER VI.

The First Four Trumpets. Revelation, chaps. vii., viii., . 78

CHAPTER VII.

Page

The Fifth and Sixth Trumpets. Revelation, chap. ix.,   95

CHAPTER VIII.

Christ appears as a Mighty Angel : the End not Yet. Revelation, chap. x., ...   109

CHAPTER IX.

The Testimony of the Witnesses—the Seventh Trumpet. Revelation, chap. xi., ...   115

CHAPTER X.

The Mystical Woman and her Seed. Revelation, chap. xii.,   125

CHAPTER XI.

Rise and Description of the Papal Beasts. Revelation, chap. xiii., ...   131

CHAPTER XII.

Daniel's Vision of the Four Beasts. Daniel chap. vii.,   .   142

CHAPTER XIII.

Sundry Visions—Preparation for the Seven Last Plagues. Revelation, chaps. xiv., xv.,   .   .   .   150

CHAPTER XIV.

The Pouring out of the Seven Vials. Revelation, chap. xvi.,   158

CHAPTER XV.

Page

God's Judgment upon the Great Whore. Revelation, chap. xvii., ... 172

CHAPTER XVI.

The Fall of the Mystical Babylon. Great Lamentation on Earth, and great Rejoicing in Heaven, on account of it. Revelation, chap. xviii., ... 179

CHAPTER XVII.

Rejoicings in Heaven over the Fall of Babylon. Revelation, chap. xix., ... 183

CHAPTER XVIII.

The Millennium. The general Resurrection and Judgment; and the final Destruction of the Wicked. Revelation, chap. xx., ... 192

CHAPTER XIX.

Glorious Destination of the Righteous—Symbolical Representation of the Church in Heaven — Conclusion. Revelation, chaps. xxi., xxii., ... 202

CHAPTER XX.

The Songs of the Apocalypse, ... 212

CHAPTER XXI.

The Lessons of the Apocalypse, ... 222

APPENDIX.

Ezekiel's Vision, ... 233

THE

APOCALYPSE EXPLAINED.

CHAPTER I.

THE APOCALYPSE ; WHEN WRITTEN, AND BY WHOM.

NO one of our sacred books has excited so many
questions, and led to such diverse interpretations, as the Apocalypse. It is not my purpose to
notice all of these, or any considerable part of
them, but I shall content myself with showing
what I conceive to be its true history, design, and
interpretation.

I begin with inquiring as to the *author* of the
book, and the *date* of it.

The Apocalypse is repeatedly said to have been
written by John. It commences with a declaration
to this effect: 'And He sent and signified it, by His
angel, to His servant *John*.' Also: '*John* to the
seven Churches of Asia.'—'I *John*, saw the Holy
City, the new Jerusalem, coming down from God
out of heaven.'

But what John was this?   Was it John the beloved disciple and apostle, or some other man? Papias speaks of a presbyter of the name of John, who lived in Asia Minor in the latter part of the first century; and by some critics, the Apocalypse has been ascribed to him.   But of this John we know little or nothing except the name; and the supposition that he wrote the Apocalypse is a mere conjecture, got up two hundred years after his death, by those who wished to destroy the canonical authority of the book.   We dismiss the suggestion, therefore, as not worthy of serious consideration, and adopt heartily the commonly received opinion, that the author of this wonderful book was no other than the apostle John.

In proof of this, we cite, first, *the circumstances of the writer*, as detailed by himself.   He says (chap. i. 9), 'I John, who also am your brother, and companion in tribulation, and in the kingdom and patience of Jesus Christ, was in the isle that is called Patmos, for the word of God, and for the testimony of Jesus Christ.'   In other words, the writer, whoever he may have been, was, at the time, suffering persecution for the truth's sake, and was in banishment on the isle of Patmos.   But, according to the united testimony of the early fathers, the apostle John, in a time of severe persecution, was banished to the isle of Patmos.   I hardly need quote their language on this point.   Clement of Alexandria, Tertullian, Origen, Victorinus, Eusebius, Epiphanius, Sulpicius Severus, Jerome, and a great many others,[1] tell us (to use the very words of Origen), 'that a Roman emperor banished the *apostle John* into the isle of Patmos, for the testimony which he bore to the word of truth.'   This shows that it was John the apostle, and not another, who wrote the book under consideration.

And to this fact, we have the direct testimony of many of the early fathers.   Justin Martyr, who flourished from forty to sixty years after the death of John, says, 'A certain man, John by name, who was one of the apostles of Christ, prophesied,' etc.[2] Melito, bishop of Sardis, a contemporary of Justin, wrote a book concerning 'the Apocalypse of John.'[3] Apollonius, a distinguished writer of Asia Minor, in a book against the Montanists, appeals, in like manner, to 'the Apocalypse of John.'[3]   Irenæus, in his work against Heresies (book 4, chapter xx.), speaks repeatedly of John—the same who wrote the gospel—as the author of the Apocalypse.   Clement of Alexandria, speaking of the righteous man, says, 'He shall sit among the twenty-four thrones, judging the people, as John saith in the Apocalypse.'[4]

---

[1] See Lardner's Credibility, vol. v. pp. 414–416.
[2] Dialogue with Trypho, chap. 80, 81.
[3] In Euseb. Ecc. Hist. iv. 24 and 28, v. 18.
[4] Strom. iv. 4.

Tertullian, the first of the Latin fathers, speaks often of the Apocalypse as the work of the apostle John. In his book against Marcion, referring to Rev. i. 16, he says, that 'the apostle John, in the Apocalypse, describes the sword proceeding from the mouth of God.'

Hippolytus, bishop of Ostia, testifies abundantly to the Johannean origin of the Apocalypse. In his book, 'De Antichristo,' section 9, he says, 'Blessed John, apostle and disciple of the Lord, tell me what thou didst see and hear respecting Babylon?' and then he quotes Revelation, chapters xvii. and xviii., as the testimony of the apostle.

Origen, the most learned of the early fathers, who was born only seventy-eight years after the death of John, speaks continually of this apostle as the author of the Apocalypse. I hardly need quote passages. In his commentary on Matthew, he says, 'John has left us one gospel. He also wrote the Apocalypse.' Again, he quotes what 'John, the son of Zebedee, says in the Apocalypse.'

But if the Apocalypse was so generally regarded, in the first ages of the Church, as the work of John, and of canonical authority, how came it to be, after a time, disputed? What could have led some of the fathers of the third and fourth centuries, as Dionysius, and Nepos of Alexandria, and Caius of Rome, and even Eusebius, the historian, to enter-

tain doubts respecting it? To this I answer: These
doubts were entertained, not at all on historical
grounds, but for reasons purely *doctrinal.* The
historical proof of the apostolical and canonical
authority of the Apocalypse was ample; but the
millenarians laid hold of a passage in the 20th
chapter—that which speaks of the binding of Satan
for a thousand years—and urged it in proof of their
peculiar sentiments. And the fathers above mentioned thought that, perhaps, the best way to be
rid of the troublesome passage was to discard the
book which contained it. Thus Luther reasoned,
for a time, in regard to the Epistle of James, because he did not know how to interpret it; he was,
at the first, inclined to reject it.

After the revolution under Constantine, the
Millenarianism of the primitive times fell into
disrepute. And from that period, the authority
of the Apocalypse was fully restored, and, with
few exceptions, has been maintained to our own
times.

During the last century, the critics of Germany
have assailed the Apocalypse, denying, in the most
positive terms, that it can have been written by
the apostle John. Thus De Wette says: 'Nothing
stands so firm as that the apostle John—if he be
the writer of the Gospel, and the first Epistle—did
not write the Apocalypse;' and Ewald says: 'That

the Apocalypse was not written by the same hand
which wrote the Gospel and the Epistle, is clear as
the light of the sun.' The principal objection to
the Johannean origin of the Apocalypse grows out
of its *style*—its *peculiar words and phrases;* an argu-
ment by which this class of critics have shown
themselves able to prove or disprove almost anything; by which they have proved that Moses did
not write the Pentateuch, nor Daniel his prophecies,
nor the Evangelists the Gospels which bear their
names; by which they have proved that Homer
did not write his poems, nor Plato his dialogues,
nor Cicero but a part of his orations.

The style of the Apocalypse is not more different
from that of the other writings of John, than is the
subject, the method, the object of the composition.
How is it possible, in writing such a book as that
before us,—made up, in great part, of visions, types,
and symbolic representations,—that the style should
not differ from that of a plain historic narrative, or
a familiar loving epistle? Any competent critic
would decide before hand that there must be
peculiar expressions, and a wide diversity of
style.

And yet there are found many characteristic re-
semblances. Professor Stuart has drawn out a long
list of these, filling several pages of his learned
commentary, showing that many of the favourite

expressions of John, occurring in his Gospels and Epistles, are also found in the Apocalypse.[1]

But if John wrote the Apocalypse, *when did he write it?* And what is the proper *date* of the book?

That John saw his visions while a persecuted exile on the isle of Patmos, he has himself declared. He either wrote them while on the island, or shortly after his return.

But when was John banished to the isle of Patmos? Under which of the emperors did his exile occur?

On this question, modern interpreters are divided, some supposing that he was exiled in the persecution under Nero about the year 66; while others insist that he was banished by Domitian·as late as the year 96. If the former of these suppositions is correct, then John was banished and saw his visions previous to the destruction of Jerusalem by Titus. And those who adopt this view insist that the greater part of the Revelation, all between the 4th and 20th chapters, relates to the approaching destruction of Jerusalem, and the death of Nero; or, at farthest, to the fall of the Pagan Roman empire.

This scheme of interpretation was first invented by the Jesuits,[2] with a view to rescue Popery from

---

[1] See Stuart's Comment. on the Apocalypse, vol. i. p. 406.

[2] By Alcazar, a Spanish Jesuit, who flourished near the commencement of the seventeenth century.

the blasting visions and denunciations of the Apocalypse. It was earnestly adopted by the Rationalists of Germany. It has since found favour with a class of interpreters in England and this country, among whom we are sorry to include the late Professor Stuart of Andover, and Professor Cowles of Oberlin. I shall go into a brief examination of this scheme of interpretation in my next chapter. At present we have merely to do with the date of the Apocalypse, or the time when it was written.

It has been thought to favour the early date of the Apocalypse, and the interpretation growing out of it, that the things therein predicted were to be fulfilled *quickly* : ' The revelation of Jesus Christ, which God gave unto Him, to show unto His servants things that *must shortly come to pass*' (Rev. i. 1.) But it is admitted by all, that, among the things predicted in this book, are, the resurrection, the general judgment, and the final state of the righteous and the wicked, and of these things it is said repeatedly in the closing chapter, that they ' *must shortly be done :*'—' The time is at hand.'—' Behold I come quickly, and my reward is with me, to give every man according as his work shall be' (Rev. xxii. 6, 10, 12).

How, then, is this phraseology to be understood? How was it understood by the author of the book and by the Spirit who indited it? Not, surely, according to our estimation of time, but rather as God estimates it, to whom 'one day is as a thousand years, and a thousand years as one day.'

It is assumed by some writers, that the coming of Christ, spoken of in Rev. i. 7, is His coming to destroy Jerusalem, because of the intimation, that some who were actually concerned in His crucifixion would be present: 'Every eye shall see Him, and *they also which pierced Him.*' But, in the sense in which the murderous Jews pierced the Saviour, we all have pierced Him by our sins. He was literally pierced by only one man, and he a Roman soldier (John xix. 34). In the same sentence with that above quoted, it is said, that ' all the kindreds of the earth shall wail because of Him' (Rev. i. 7). Were 'all the kindreds of the earth' present, with their wailings and lamentations, when Jerusalem was destroyed? or, is this scene reserved to the final coming of Christ to judge the world?

It is further urged, that the Apocalypse must have been written as early as the time of Nero, since only seven Churches are mentioned in it, which, probably, was the whole number at that time existing in Asia Minor. But it would be easy to show that there were many Churches in Asia Minor before the deaths of Peter and Paul. In addition to those addressed in the Apocalypse, there

B

were Churches certainly in Iconium, in Lystra, in Derbe, in the Pisidian Antioch, in Hierapolis, in Pontus, in Cappadocia, in Bythinia, in Cilicia, in Galatia, in Colosse, and probably in many other places. Why messages were sent to only seven of these Churches, I pretend not to say. Perhaps these were the only ones with which John was particularly acquainted; or the number, seven, may have been taken, because it was a favourite perfect number among the Jews.

On the whole, we find nothing, in the Apocalypse or out of it, which should lead us to think that it was written during the persecution under Nero, and that the most of it relates to his death and to the destruction of Jerusalem, or to the fall of Pagan Rome. We adopt the other supposition; that it was written during the persecution under Domitian, near the close of the first century, and that it takes a much wider range of signification than that referred to.

It does not appear that John could have become domiciliated among the Churches of Asia Minor until near the close of the Neronian persecution. These Churches had been chiefly planted by Paul, and were under his particular care and inspection. He often visited them while he had his liberty; and after his confinement, he frequently wrote letters to, and kept up a constant communication with them; yet, in none of his letters, even to the last, do we find any mention of John, or any reference to him as residing in that quarter. Accordingly, Professor Schaff says: 'It was probably the martyrdom of the apostle to the Gentiles, and the attendant dangers and distractions, that led John to take this important step, and build his structure on the foundation laid by Paul.'[1] Neander also says: 'After the martyrdom of Paul, it is probable that John was called upon by the better part of the Churches to transfer the seat of his activity to this quarter.'[2]

Nero put an end to his life, and the persecution ceased in the year 68. Some two or three years after the death of Paul, John would hardly have removed to Asia Minor during the violence of this persecution; and he must have resided there some considerable time before he had become intimately acquainted with the Churches, and acquired such an influence and authority, as would justify him in directing such messages to them as we find in the Revelation. The probability therefore is, that John was not in Asia Minor, or, if there, was not in circumstances to present them with such a book as that before us, until long after Nero was dead, and his bitter persecution of the Christians had ceased.

[1] Hist. of Apostolic Churches, p. 399.
[2] Planting and training the Apostolic Churches, p. 219.

A variety of evidence, drawn from the Apocalypse itself, goes to assure us that it could not have been written until near the close of the first century.

It was not till this time that the first day of the week began to be called 'the Lord's day,' yet it was on 'the Lord's day' that John was in the Spirit, and saw the opening vision of the Apocalypse (Rev. i. 10).

It was not till near the close of the first century that there was a presiding elder, an angel, in each of the Churches. Previous to this the elders of a Church were always classed together, but each of the seven Churches of Asia seems to have had a presiding officer, or elder, when the Apocalypse was written.

The Gnostic errors had begun to show themselves in the time of Paul, but they had not been matured and organised under heresiarchs before the close of the first century; yet we hear of the Nicolaitanes, a sect of Gnostics, in two of the messages to the Churches of Asia (Rev. ii. 6, 15). Near the close of the first century, and not earlier, the Gnostic leaders commenced the work of mutilating the sacred books of the Christians. It was this practice, probably, which led to the closing denunciations of the Apocalypse: 'If any man shall add unto these things, God shall add unto him the plagues that are written in this book: and if any man shall take away from the words of the book of this prophecy, God shall take away his part out of the book of life, and out of the holy city, and from the things that are written in this book.' There had been no occasion for language such as this until near the close of the first century.

It is obvious that the seven Churches of Asia were in a very different condition, when the Apocalypse was written, from what they were in the time of Nero and of Paul. The Church at Ephesus had 'lost its first love.' The Church at Smyrna had those in its communion who belonged to 'the synagogue of Satan.' The Church at Pergamos harboured not only the Nicolaitanes, but those who held 'the doctrine of Balaam, who taught Balak to cast a stumbling-block before the children of Israel.' The Church at Thyatira suffered 'the woman Jezebel' to teach, to seduce its members to commit fornication, and to eat things sacrificed to idols. The Church at Sardis had only 'a few names' left which had not defiled their garments; while the members of the Church at Laodicea had become so lukewarm and offensive to Christ, that He was ready to 'spue them out of His mouth.'

In short, these Churches had all of them declined—sadly declined, from what they were when Paul wrote his Epistles to some of them; and *time must be allowed—a considerable time*, in which to account for their defections. If we suppose the

Apocalypse written during the persecution under Nero,—only a few years subsequent to the writing of Paul's Epistles,—the requisite time is not furnished. But if the book was written thirty years later, in the persecution under Domitian, the declension can be accounted for, at least on the score of time.

The testimony of the Fathers on the point before us is just what, in view of the facts above detailed, we might expect. With few exceptions, it is unanimous in ascribing the exile of John, and the writing of the Apocalypse, to the time of Domitian. We commence with Irenæus, bishop of Lyons, in Gaul. He had been a disciple of Polycarp, who was a disciple of the apostle John. He must have been familiarly acquainted with the circumstances of John's banishment, with the time of it, and the person by whom it had been decreed. He could not have been mistaken on these points, nor is there any mistake or ambiguity in his testimony. 'The Apocalypse,' he tells us, was seen *not long ago*, but *almost in our own generation, near the end of the reign of Domitian.*[1] This testimony has never been set aside, and never can be. It is enough of itself, considering the circumstances, to decide the question before us.

But this testimony does not stand alone. It is concurred in by nearly all the more distinguished

[1] Contra Hæres, v. 20.

Fathers. Victorinus says repeatedly, that John was banished by Domitian, and in his time saw the Revelation. Hippolytus speaks of John as having been exiled to Patmos under Domitian, where he saw the Apocalypse.[1] Eusebius, speaking of the persecution, says: 'In this persecution, John the apostle and evangelist, being still alive, was banished into the isle of Patmos.'[2] Jerome, in his book of illustrious men, says: 'Domitian, in the fourteenth year of his reign, raised the next persecution after Nero, when John was banished to the isle of Patmos, where he wrote the Revelation.' In another work, he says: 'John was a prophet. He saw the Revelation in the isle of Patmos, where he was banished by Domitian.'[3] Sulpicius Severus says, that 'John, the apostle and evangelist, was banished by Domitian to the isle of Patmos, where he had visions, and where he wrote the Revelation.'[4]

It would be needless to multiply quotations like these, and pursue them to a later period. It has been said that these testimonies are of little value, since they are all based one upon another, and ultimately upon that of Irenæus. But this is not true; at least, no one has any right or reason to affirm that it is true. They go to show what was

[1] Works, p. 90.
[2] Ecc. Hist. Lib. 3, cap. 18.
[3] Works, vol. vi. p. 446.
[4] Works, vol. iv. chap. 120.

the settled conviction of the Church on the point before us, from the second century to the sixth,—the very time when the question could best be settled; and, in the judgment then formed, and so unanimously expressed, it becomes us of the nineteenth century to acquiesce. It cannot be reversed but upon vastly weightier reasons than any that have yet been urged.

It will be seen that the question here discussed has a vital bearing on the interpretation of the Apocalypse. If this book was written near the close of the first century, almost thirty years after the death of Nero and the fall of Jerusalem, then it is vain to look for its fulfilment in either of these events. There is not the slightest allusion to either of them, from one end of the book to the other.

But as many persons at this day,—following Professor Stuart and the Germans,—are inclined to adopt their scheme of interpretation, it may be well to examine it more particularly.

CHAPTER II.

REVIEW OF PROFESSOR STUART ON THE APOCALYPSE:

WITH OCCASIONAL REFERENCES TO THE COMMENTARY OF PROFESSOR COWLES.

AMONG my ministerial friends who have passed away, no one stood higher than the late Professor Moses Stuart of Andover. I loved and honoured him while he lived, and venerate his memory now that he is gone. He was the father of biblical learning in this country. He did more to promote a knowledge of the original Scriptures, especially those of the Old Testament, than any other individual. On most of his exegetical writings I set a high value, and it is with pain that I feel constrained to differ from him in regard to any of them. But his learned, laboured, exhaustive work on the Apocalypse I consider the least valuable of his Commentaries. The plan of this Commentary, borrowed mostly from the Germans, is founded on a false assumption; and this fact vitiates, confuses, and half spoils the whole.

Professor Stuart assumes that the Apocalypse was written about the year 68, just before the

C

death of Nero, and two years previous to the destruction of Jerusalem by Titus.

In the Apocalypse, we have set before us, he says, three distinct catastrophes:

1. The fall of Jerusalem, in chapters vi.–xi.

2. The fall of Nero, and ultimately of Pagan Rome, in chapters xii.–xix.

3. The overthrow of Gog and Magog, after the close of the millennium.

There is no reference to Papal Rome anywhere. The prophetic symbols, from the beginning of the sixth chapter to the close of the eleventh, all relate to the destruction of Jerusalem. Those from the twelfth to the nineteenth, to the fall of Nero and of Pagan Rome. The principal reasons assigned for referring all the debatable parts of the Apocalypse to the former two of these catastrophes, are the following :—

1. On any other supposition, the symbols of the Apocalypse would not have been understood by those to whom the book was addressed, nor even by John himself.

This consideration seems to have had great weight in the mind of Professor Stuart, and also of Professor Cowles, as both writers refer to it often, and in various connections. Let us then inquire, for a moment, how much it is likely that John understood of the Apocalypse at the time when he was receiving and writing it.

John knew what he saw in vision—the symbols, pictures, and images that were presented. He knew what he heard said and sung among the celestials. He knew enough, to record what he had seen and heard in plain intelligible language. But did he know to what particular events the symbols which he employed—the horsemen, the locusts, the beasts, the trumpets, the vials, etc., referred—what they were designed to represent, so that he could have written out a clear and full explication of them? I doubt it. It is not at all likely that he had such an understanding as this of what he was writing. Nor was such knowledge on his part at all necessary to accomplish his object in preparing the work, or the object of the Spirit in enabling him to prepare it. This was, to comfort the afflicted persecuted people of God with the assurance, that all heaven was in sympathy with them in their trials, and that they were sure to end in victory and peace. Such was the immediate object of the Apocalypse; and this could be as well answered without a particular understanding of the significance of each of the symbols, as with it.

It is in this way that the book has been a light and a comfort to the Church in all succeeding ages. Christians have not known—in general they have not pretended to know, the particular significance of the symbols. Yet they have derived much instruction and comfort from the book.

Indeed, the knowledge of the ancient prophets, in predicting the Messiah and the way of salvation through Him, did not extend much farther than has been here represented; for we are told that they searched diligently ' what, or what manner of time, the Spirit of Christ which was in them did signify, when it testified beforehand the sufferings of Christ, and the glory that should follow' (1 Pet. i. 11).

And, so far as John understood his writings, I suppose the Churches to which they were addressed understood them, and no further. They knew what John had written, what things he had described, and the meaning of his words. But did their knowledge extend much beyond this? I think not. Further knowledge was not necessary to their encouragement and comfort; and judging from the specimens which we have of the explications and comments of the early Christians, we cannot give them much credit for their knowledge of the Apocalypse. They early began to allegorize it after the fashion of the times. They appealed to it in support of their millenarian views, which had begun to prevail before the Apocalypse was written. And of all the wild vagaries that have ever been written on this book, some of their interpretations were the wildest. Take, for example, the comments of Hippolytus on Rev. xii. 'The woman is the Church; the sun which encompasses her means the Word of God; the moon under her feet indicates that her splendour is celestial. The crown of twelve stars indicates the twelve apostles; the woes of parturiency show that the Church at all times is bringing forth the Word of God, which suffers persecution by the world. By the two eagles' wings given to the woman, in order to aid her flight, we are to understand belief in Christ, who, on the cross, spread out His two hands like wings for a protection to His followers.' This will do as a specimen of patristic interpretation.

2. Professor Stuart, and others who follow him, endeavour to support their theory by certain representations of the Apocalypse, which,—though in the midst of symbols, and themselves manifestly symbolical,—it is insisted must be understood literally.

Thus, because the 144,000 sealed ones in Rev. vii. are said to be taken from the twelve tribes of Israel, it is thought that they include none but believing Jews,—the same that took warning and fled from Jerusalem when the city was destroyed. But do not these interpreters know that the whole Christian Church is called in Scripture 'the Israel of God,' though a vast majority of its members are not, and, since the first century, never have been converted Jews? As well might it be inferred, since the names of 'the twelve tribes of Israel' are inscribed over the gates of the celestial city, chapter xxi. 12, that none but converted Jews can ever pass through them into heaven.

If the passage before us is to be understood literally, then, not only were 144,000 converted Jews sealed, but 12,000 were sealed from each of the twelve tribes. Now, does any one believe such a statement as this? Professor Stuart did not believe it.[1] Clearly the passage is to be understood, not literally, but symbolically; and thus understood, it is easy of interpretation.

In Rev. xi. 1, 2, John says, that there was given him a reed, and he was commanded to rise and measure the temple of God, and the altar, and them that worship therein. 'But the court that is without the temple leave out, and measure it not; for it is given unto the Gentiles. And the holy city shall they tread under foot forty and two months.' From this, it is confidently affirmed, that the temple at Jerusalem was standing when the passage was written.

The whole question resolves itself into this: Is this passage to be understood literally, or symbolically? If literally, then John, on the isle of Patmos, in the Ægean sea, was commanded to take a measuring-rod and hie away to the literal Jerusalem,

[1] See Commentary, vol. ii. p. 173.

and measure the temple, and the altar, and them that worship therein! And now, I ask, Who believes this? Who can believe it? But this is not all. In measuring the temple and the altar, John was to leave out the court of the temple, and not measure it; for this was given to the Gentiles to be trodden under foot. According to this, interpreted literally, the Romans were not to destroy the temple itself, but only the court; whereas it is certain that they did destroy the entire temple, court and all, leaving not one stone upon another.

What then are we to say of the representation in Rev. xi. 1, 2? Is it to be understood literally or symbolically? Literally, it cannot be understood. So says Professor Stuart himself.[1] But symbolically understood, the interpretation is easy. The temple and the holy city signify the Church of God, which was to be persecuted and trodden down of the wicked for a given time, but ultimately was to be delivered, and to triumph.

It is further said, that the two witnesses spoken of in this chapter, must have been slain in the literal Jerusalem, because their dead bodies are said to ' lie in the street of the great city, which spiritually is called Sodom and Egypt, where also our Lord was crucified.' Upon this, I have only to ask, Are Sodom and Egypt to be understood literally?

[1] Vol. ii. p. 213.

And if not, why is Jerusalem to be taken literally? And if the whole passage is to be understood symbolically, as it certainly must be, then it furnishes no more evidence that the literal Jerusalem was standing when John wrote the Apocalypse, than that the literal Sodom was.

3. Professor Stuart claims credit for his theory of the Apocalypse, on account of the absurd explications which have been given on the commonly received theory. 'Men have regarded the Apocalypse as a prophetic syllabus of all civil and ecclesiastical history, from the author's time to the end of the world.'

We admit that a great many absurd and foolish things have been said by commentators, though we doubt whether any have gone so far as Professor Stuart represents, making the Apocalypse a syllabus of *all* civil and ecclesiastical history. But have there not been as absurd explications by Germans and Roman Catholics, who in general adopt the theory of Professor Stuart? It would be easy to show as much as this, without looking beyond the pages of Stuart's Commentary.

Professors Stuart and Cowles think to avoid such absurdities, by saying that most of the symbols which John employs have no particular significance. They are the mere dress and furniture of the poem. The seals and the trumpets mean nothing, except that Jerusalem was to be destroyed, as besieged cities commonly are, by the sword, the famine, and pestilence.

In a few instances, however, these men venture upon the interpretation of symbols; and, we doubt, whether explications more absurd were ever uttered. As before remarked, Professor Stuart makes the beast, whose head was wounded to death, and afterwards healed, to be Nero ; because some of the old heathen soothsayers had a groundless prediction, that when Nero died he would be restored to life. And Professor Cowles interprets the seventh trumpet,—on the sounding of which 'great voices were heard in heaven saying, The kingdoms of this world are become the kingdoms of our Lord and of His Christ,'—as denoting the destruction of Jerusalem !! ' The seventh angel's trump involves this; nothing less, nothing more,' p. 138.   His only reason for this interpretation is, that his theory demands it. Jerusalem must be destroyed just at this point, and the seventh trumpet must denote it.

My objections to Professor Stuart's scheme of interpretation—and that of Professor Cowles is much the same—are, in brief, as follows :—

1. He represents his first catastrophe—the destruction of Jerusalem—as being described in Rev. chapter xi.; whereas, in truth, there is no catastrophe there.   Let any reader look over the chapter,

D

and see if he can find it.   There is first the measuring of the mystical temple, signifying the Church, and a leaving out of the court, which is given to the Gentiles, who are to tread down the holy city—another symbol of God's living Church—forty and two months.   Then follows the testimony of the witnesses in sack-cloth, their death, and their resurrection.   This resurrection probably took place at the time of the reformation from Popery, when there were mighty changes in the Roman earth—all prefigured by an earthquake, and the fall of the tenth part of the city—the Popish hierarchy.   That the city here spoken of, a tenth part of which fell, cannot be the literal Jerusalem, is evident from the fact, that Jerusalem was *totally* destroyed by the Romans shortly after the earthquake of the Reformation. The seventh trumpet sounds, and the millennial period is announced.   Such is a brief analysis of this chapter; and where in it are we to look for any such great catastrophe as the destruction of Jerusalem by the Romans? I cannot find it; nor do I believe any sober interpreter can.

2. But if there be such a catastrophe here as Professor Stuart represents, it ought to be called the second, and not the first.   The second catastrophe, pertaining to Nero, is in the 19th chapter. But Nero was slain at least two years before Jerusalem was destroyed,—in which time there reigned

no less than four emperors. Nero is supposed to have died in the year 68; but Jerusalem was destroyed, under Vespasian, in the year 70. Why then, we ask, was the first catastrophe made the second, and the second the first? Why were not these events predicted, if predicted at all, in the order of time?

3. The symbols of destruction in the Revelation, which Professor Stuart refers to Jerusalem, are said by the writer to apply to the *whole earth*—that is, the Roman earth. Thus, power was given to him that sat on the red horse to take peace from *the earth*. And power was given unto him on the pale horse ' over the fourth part of *the earth*, to kill with the sword, and with hunger, and with the beasts of the earth' (chap. vi. 4, 8). And when the first trumpet sounded, there followed hail and fire, mingled with blood, and they were cast upon *the earth* (chap. viii. 7). In Asia Minor, in the last half of the first century, the term *earth* could never have been understood as referring to the little and remote province of Judea. It must have meant the Roman empire.

4. Those who were smitten by the blast of the sixth trumpet,—some of whom were slain, and some spared,—could not have been Jews; since they are expressly said to have been idolaters. ' The rest of the men that were not killed by these

plagues yet repented not of the works of their
hands, that they should not worship devils, and
idols of gold, and silver, and brass, and stone, and
of wood: which can neither hear, nor see, nor
walk' (chap. ix. 20).   How is it possible to apply
this passage to the Jews, who were not idolaters?'

5. In the same chapter (ix.), the number of
horsemen drawn together to the battle, and drawn
from the East—the region of the Euphrates—is
two hundred thousand thousand.   Was any such
army, or any thing like it, or any army at all,
drawn from the region of the Euphrates to fight
against Jerusalem at the time of its overthrow.
Let those who have read the history decide.

6. The woman described in chapter xii., Professors Stuart and Cowles both take to be the virgin
Mary, giving birth to the Saviour of the world,
and then fleeing to her hiding-place in Egypt;
thus looking backward a period of seventy years,
and not forward, as a prophet should do, into the
future.   And why should this little scrap of history—if it be history—be thrown in here, in connection with the destruction of Jerusalem?

7. This scheme of interpretation makes a long
stride from the fall of Nero in the first century, or
of Pagan Rome in the time of Constantine, to the
incoming of the millennium.   Of all the intervening
space,—so full of incident and of interest to the

Church of God,—the writer of the Apocalypse is thought to take not the slightest notice. On any theory of interpretation, would not this be regarded as a strange fact, and a strong objection?

8. But my principal objection to Professor Stuart's interpretation of the Apocalypse is, that he has fixed upon a wrong time for the writing of the book, and this vitiates and nullifies all his reasonings on the subject. We have shown, we think conclusively, that this book was written, not' during the persecution under Nero, but thirty years later, in the time of Domitian—long after Nero was dead and Jerusalem destroyed. And this changes the whole aspect and import of the book. Instead of being filled up with symbols and predictions in regard to these two events, there is not the slightest reference to either of them, as I have before remarked, in all that the Apostle has written.

CHAPTER III.

THE FIRST THREE CHAPTERS CONSIDERED.

REVELATION, CHAPS I., II., III.

PATMOS, the place of John's banishment, is a
desolate island in the Ægean sea, lying between Icaria and the promontory of Miletus. It is
some six or eight miles in length, but its average
breadth is scarcely more than one mile. It has no
trees or rivers, and very little land that is capable
of cultivation. Owing to its isolated and desolate
character, it was frequently used by the Romans as
a place of banishment for criminals.

During his exile on this dreary spot, the venerable Apostle was not entirely deserted. In the
absence of earthly friends and comforts, he seems
to have enjoyed the most precious communion with
Christ, and the most glorious manifestations or
visions of His presence. We have a glowing account of one of these visions,—perhaps the first of
them,—in the first chapter of the Revelation. It
occurred, like the Pentecost, on the first day of the
week—'the Lord's day,' thus putting a new honour
upon what was to be the Sabbath of the Christian
dispensation. 'I was in the Spirit on the Lord's

day, and I heard behind me a great voice, as of a trumpet, saying, I am Alpha and Omega, the first and the last: and, What thou seest, write in a book, and send it unto the seven Churches which are in Asia . . . And I turned to see the voice that spake with me. And, being turned, I saw seven golden candlesticks; and in the midst of the seven candle-sticks one like unto the Son of man, clothed with a garment down to the foot, and girt about the paps with a golden girdle. His head and his hairs were white like wool, as white as snow; and his eyes were as a flame of fire; and his feet like unto fine brass, as if they burned in a furnace; and his voice as the sound of many waters. And he had in his right hand seven stars; and out his mouth went a sharp two-edged sword; and his countenance was as the sun shineth in his strength.' Such was the appearance of the glorified Son of God, manifesting himself to His suffering disciple on this memorable occasion.

After the first surprise of His appearance had passed away, Christ proceeds to give to John His commission to *write the book of Revelation*, the very book on which we are commenting. And in the commission itself, a threefold division of the book is indicated. 'Write,' says He, '*the things which thou hast seen; and the things which are*, and *the things which shall be hereafter.*'

According to the division here indicated, the first part of the book is comprised in the first chapter. For here is the record which John made of the resplendent and glorious vision which he had witnessed. I have no occasion to remark particularly on this part of the book.

The second part of the book,—'the things which *are*,'—is comprised in the second and third chapters. Here we have the messages of instruction and warning which were to be sent to the seven Churches in Asia. This part of the book is not prophetical at all. It is simply a record of the things which *are*.

My plan does not require me to go into a particular explanation of this second part of the book. And yet, considering the interest and importance of these messages of love—addressed primarily to the Churches of Asia, but recorded for the benefit of all the Churches,—I cannot consent to pass from them without a few general remarks.

1. Though intended for the *Churches* to which they were addressed, they are all directed to the *angels* of these Churches. By these angels of the Churches, we are to understand, I think, their principal pastors. In all the large Churches planted by the apostles, there were, at the first, several presbyters or elders. Such were the elders of the Church at Jerusalem, and of the Church at Ephesus.

When these elders met together for business or devotion, they would need some one to be their moderator or president. By the close of the first century, the presiding elder had come to be regarded as a standing officer, and in process of time appropriated to himself the name of bishop. It was in this way that the distinction between bishop and presbyter crept into the Church,—a distinction entirely unknown in the days of the apostles. These presiding elders were, I suppose, the angels of the Churches in Asia, to whom the messages of the Saviour were primarily directed.

2. These messages were all prefaced by mentioning some of the appearances, doings, or attributes of the glorified Saviour—those which, in the first chapter, had been ascribed to Him. Thus, in the epistle to the Church at Ephesus, He is said to hold ' the stars in His right hand,' and to walk ' in the midst of the seven golden candlesticks;' in the epistle to the Church at Smyrna, He is 'the first and the last, which was dead and is alive;' in the epistle to the Church at Pergamos, He 'hath the sharp sword with two edges;' in the epistle to the Church at Thyatira, He 'hath his eyes like a flame of fire, and his feet like fine brass;' in the epistle to the Church at Sardis, He 'hath the seven Spirits of God, and the seven stars;' in the epistle to the Church at Philadelphia, He is 'He that is holy, He

E

that is true, He that hath the key of David, He that openeth, and no man shutteth, and shutteth, and no man openeth;' in the epistle to the Church at Laodicea, He 'is the Amen, the faithful and true witness, the beginning of the creation of God.'[1] These several prefaces are all adapted to arrest attention, and make an impression; and it may be that each was selected with special reference to the state of the particular Church.

3. These introductions are followed, in every instance, with the startling announcement, '*I know thy works.*' Yes! whether faithful or unfaithful, warm or lukewarm, heretical or otherwise, true or false, your case is all open to Him with whom you have to do: '*I know thy works.*'

4. These epistles are messages of mingled commendation and reproof, in bestowing which the speaker is eminently pungent, direct, and faithful, —like one speaking with authority from heaven. In the Churches at Sardis and Laodicea, the Saviour finds little or nothing to commend; in the Churches at Smyrna and Philadelphia, He finds little to reprove; while, in the remaining three, there are some things to be commended, and others to be censured.

5. In administering reproof, these epistles are

---

[1] Αρχη, the *head*, the *governor* of the creation, the *prime efficient* of it.

patterns of heavenly wisdom, tenderness, and fidelity, which cannot be too closely studied and imitated by all who are called to the discharge of this painful duty. Take, for example, the Church at Ephesus. The Saviour commences by praising this Church; and He continues His commendations as though He could never stop, 'I know thy works, and thy labour, and thy patience, and how thou canst not bear them that are evil, and thou hast tried them which say they are apostles, and are not, and hast found them liars; and hast borne, and hast patience, and for my name's sake hast laboured, and hast not fainted.' Having said as much as this, the speaker can now proceed and say anything. He cannot possibly give offence by anything which will be likely to follow. 'Nevertheless, I have somewhat against thee, because thou hast left thy first love.' When will reprovers and reformers learn to deal with delinquents after this manner? How much reproof is worse than wasted, by the indulgence of a different spirit, and by pursuing a different course?

6. These epistles are filled up with earnest exhortations to repentance and reformation, with the richest promises in case of amendment, and with the most terrific denunciations upon those who persist in evil. 'Remember, therefore, from whence thou art fallen, and repent, and do the first works.' 'Re-

pent, or else I will come unto thee quickly, and will fight against thee with the sword of my mouth.' 'Be watchful, and strengthen the things which remain, that are ready to die.' 'To him that overcometh will I grant to sit with me in my throne, even as I also overcame, and am set down with my Father in His throne.'

7. Considering the Author of these warnings, exhortations, and promises, and the circumstances under which they were uttered, we are not surprised to hear each message close with the declaration: 'He that hath an ear, let him hear what the Spirit saith unto the Churches.'

May each one of *us* regard this solemn declaration as addressed particularly to ourselves. God has given us not only ears to hear, but means and advantages for understanding and improvement. Let us then hear these words of the Spirit to the Churches, and heed and obey them, that we may be heirs of the precious promises contained in them, and be prepared for the blessings which Christ has in store for all His people.

CHAPTER IV.

INTRODUCTION TO THE PROPHETICAL PORTION.

REVELATION CHAPS. IV., V.

IN my last chapter, I reviewed the first three chapters of the Revelation, containing an account of the writer's first vision on Patmos,—a vision of the glorified Son of God; together with His messages to the seven Churches of Asia. In the commission to John to write this book, I have said that a threefold division of it was indicated by the Saviour. John was to write the things which *he had seen*, the things which *are*, and those which *shall be hereafter*. The two first of these divisions are included in the chapters already considered. The third part of the book—the *prophetical* part—commences properly with the sixth chapter. The fourth and fifth chapters—in which is presented a bright vision of heaven—may be regarded as introductory to the third or prophetical part. To these two chapters I shall now call attention.

In the commencement of the fourth chapter, John tells us that he 'looked, and, behold, a door was opened in heaven: and the first voice which I heard was as it were of a trumpet talking with me;

which said, Come up hither, and I will show the
things which must be hereafter. And immediately
I was in the Spirit; and, behold, a throne was set
in heaven, and one sat on the throne. And His
appearance was like to that of a jasper, or a sardine
stone; and there was a rainbow round about the
throne, in sight like unto an emerald.'

The personage whom John saw sitting on the
throne was, undoubtedly, the eternal Father,—the
grand executive head of the Divine administration,—
whose office-work it is to guard the honours of the
eternal throne. The rainbow round about the throne
was a bow of promise, indicating that the throne of
the Eternal is One, not only of judgment, but of grace.
John 'saw seven lamps of fire burning before the
throne, which are the seven spirits of God.' This I
understand to be a symbolic representation of the
Holy Spirit. The Hebrews regarded seven as a
perfect number. Hence the seven lamps, or seven
spirits, denote God's Holy Spirit.

John also saw 'round about the throne four and
twenty seats, and upon the seats four and twenty
elders sitting, clothed in white raiment, and having
on their heads crowns of gold.' He saw, also, four
living creatures—improperly translated in our Bibles
'beasts'—'full of eyes before and behind' (chap. iv.
4–9).

It is generally understood that the four and

twenty elders are representatives of the redeemed Church in heaven. But 'the living creatures,' who are they, and what do they represent? In appearance, they are like 'the living creatures' which Ezekiel and Isaiah saw in the commencement of their prophetic visions, and which are called cherubim and seraphim. I have no doubt that 'the living creatures' of the Apocalypse may properly be called cherubim. But what are cherubim? We have frequent mention of them and their doings in the Old Testament. Thus, when our first parents were expelled from the garden of Eden, there were 'placed, on the east of it, cherubim and a flaming sword, which turned every way to keep the way of the tree of life' (Gen. iii. 24). The cherubim that Ezekiel saw are represented as bearing up the throne of God, and as constituting, by their wings and wheels, the chariot of His glory (Ezek. i. 26 ; x. 1). It is said of the God of Israel, in the eighteenth Psalm : 'He rode upon a cherub, and did fly ; he did fly upon the wings of the wind.'

Of the symbolical import of the cherubim, various opinions have been entertained. By Mr Hutchinson and his followers, they were regarded as emblematical of the Trinity. But this idea is too absurd to require consideration. The God of Israel is always represented as distinct from the cherubim. He is served and worshipped by them.

He dwelt 'between the cherubim,' and could not have been represented by these symbols.

Some have thought that the cherubim were symbolical representations of the *powers and processes of nature,*—those through which God is carrying into effect His providential designs. But I cannot be of this opinion. They are not personifications, but personal beings. Personal offices and acts are ascribed to them. They unite with other personal beings in singing praises to God and the Lamb (See Isa. vi. 3; Rev. v. 8–11).

And not only are they personal beings, but *heavenly* beings. Their home is in heaven. Their work and worship are near the eternal throne.

Are they, then, a distinct *class* of heavenly beings; or are they a superior *order* of existing classes—holy angels and redeemed souls? I incline to the latter opinion. We know of but two distinct classes of heavenly beings,—angels and glorified men. Yet among these, we read of different orders,—some higher and some lower; some near the throne, and others at a greater distance from it. There are 'principalities and powers in heavenly places.' There are angels and archangels, cherubim and seraphim. And of those who have gone from earth to heaven, some are farther advanced than others; since every one is to be rewarded according to his works.

The cherubim and seraphim, I think, are among the highest order of celestial beings—perhaps the very highest—who stand nearest the Eternal, and are specially the servants of His throne.

All the holy angels are, indeed, the servants of God. They fly on His errands of mercy and of judgment. They 'do His commandments, hearkening unto the voice of His word.' Yet some may be more specially so than others, standing nearer to God, and engaged more directly in His service ; and this, as it seems to me, is true of the cherubim. They are emphatically the *servants of God's throne.*

And this agrees with all that we hear of them in the Scriptures. In the Jewish tabernacle and temple, where were figures of cherubim, their place was close by the glorious Shekinah—the visible manifestation of the presence of the Most High. And when Isaiah 'saw the Lord sitting upon His throne, high and lifted up, above it stood the seraphim, crying one to another, Holy, holy, holy is the Lord God of hosts.' The cherubim which Ezekiel saw were in a still more obvious attitude of service. As I just now said, they are represented as bearing up the throne of God, and as constituting the chariot of His glory. The Psalmist represents the Almighty as riding upon a cherub—

> ' On church and on cherubim
> Full royally He rode.'

F

In the Revelation, too, the living creatures, the cherubim, are represented as having their places '*in the midst of the throne, and round about it.*'

That this place of honour is occupied, and has been from the beginning, by a superior order of angels, is indubitable. But is it occupied by the angels only? Or do a portion of the *ransomed ones* share with them in this service and honour? But for a single passage,—and that one in the chapters we are considering,—we might feel constrained to answer this question in the negative. In the vision before us, ' the living creatures,' the cherubim, who are ' in the midst of the throne, and round about,' unite with the four and twenty elders in singing the new song of redeeming mercy (chap. iv. 10, 11). And when the Lamb had taken the book out of the hands of Him that sat upon the throne, ' the four living creatures, and the four and twenty elders, fell down before the Lamb, . . . and they sung a new song, saying, Thou art worthy to take the book, and to open the seals thereof; for thou wast slain, and hast redeemed us to God by Thy blood, out of every kindred, and tongue, and people, and nation' (chap. v. 9).

There is no evading the force of this passage. The living creatures, the cherubim, do here unite with the other representatives of the ransomed Church, in singing the song of redeeming mercy—

a song which none can ever learn but those who have been redeemed from among men. (See Rev. xiv. 3.) This passage, therefore, which has long been a puzzle to commentators, and which many have tried to explain away, I regard as a glorious revelation. It assures us of the high honour which is put upon the saints, or upon a portion of them, in the heavenly world. Our Saviour tells us that ' they shall be *as* the angels,' and ' *equal* to the angels ;' but we are here informed that they are to be numbered with cherubim and seraphim,—among the highest order of celestial spirits, who stand nearest the Eternal, and are emphatically the servants of His throne.

The faces and forms of these cherubim have commonly been considered,—and, I think, justly,—as indicative of their characters, their properties, their powers. The first was like a lion, to indicate their courage and power; the second was like a calf, or young ox, to indicate their patience of labour; the third had the face of a man, to indicate their intelligence; and the fourth was like a flying eagle, to indicate the rapidity of their motions in accomplishing the service of God. They were also furnished with wings, and 'were full of eyes before and behind,—still further to indicate the properties we have ascribed to them.

But without dwelling longer on the living crea-

tures, the cherubim, let us proceed to the remaining parts of the vision under consideration.

John saw 'in the right hand of Him that sat
upon the throne a book written within and on the
back side, sealed with seven seals.' And he saw 'a
strong angel proclaiming with a loud voice, Who is
worthy to open the book, and to loose the seals
thereof? And no man in heaven, nor in earth,
neither under the earth, was able to open the book,
neither to look thereon' (chap. v. 1–3).

This book which John saw was not enclosed in
covers, like our books. It was a great roll of parchment, closely rolled up, and sealed with seven seals;
so that when one seal was broken, it could be un-
rolled a certain way, to disclose what was behind it;
and when another seal was broken, it could be un-
rolled farther, to disclose more. This was the book
of prophecy—the book of God's inscrutable purposes—into which no created being in heaven, or
on earth, or anywhere else, was able to look.

And John says, 'I wept much, because no one
was found able to open the book, neither to look
thereon. And one of the elders said unto me, Weep
not; for, behold, the Lion of the tribe of Judah,
and the Root of David, hath prevailed to open the
book, and to loose the seven seals thereof' (chap. v.
4, 5).

Here the Lord Jesus Christ, 'the lion of the

tribe of Judah, and the root of David,' is first
brought upon the heavenly scene. He comes forward in appearance as a lamb that had been slain,
and takes the book out of the hands of Him that
sat upon the throne. He breaks the stubborn seals,
unrols the mystic scroll, and shows the prophetic
symbols that are concealed behind it (chap. v. 6, 7).

We have here, I must say in passing, one of the
most conclusive proofs in the Bible of the proper
divinity of our Lord Jesus Christ. No created
being in heaven, or on earth, or anywhere else,
could break one of these seals, or disclose what
was concealed under it. In other words, no created
being in the universe can look out into the distant,
contingent future, and tell us what shall be hereafter. But Christ can do this infallibly; thus prov-
ing His claim to a proper divinity.

And when the Lamb had taken the book, ' the
four living creatures, and the four and twenty
elders fell down before Him, having every one of
them harps, and golden vials full of odours,' or incense, ' which are the prayers of saints,'—or which
represent the prayers of saints. ' And they sung
a new song, saying, Thou art worthy to take the
book and to open the seals thereof, for Thou wast
slain, and hast redeemed us unto God by Thy blood,
out of every kindred, and tongue, and people, and
nation, and hast made us kings and priests unto

God, and we shall reign upon the earth' (chap. v. 8–10).

This song, as I said before, was sung by the representatives of the redeemed Church in heaven. It could be sung by no one else. The great choir of angels stood silently by, while this part of the heavenly service was performed.

But when the new song had been sung by the ransomed ones, a grand chorus was introduced, in which saints and angels—the entire host of heaven —could all unite. 'I beheld,' says John, 'and I heard the voice of many angels round about the throne, and the living creatures and the elders, and the number of them was ten thousand times ten thousand, and thousands of thousands, saying, with a loud voice, Worthy is the Lamb that was slain to receive power, and riches, and wisdom, and strength, and honour, and glory, and blessing. And every creature which is in heaven, and on the earth, and under the earth, and such as are in the sea, and all that are in them, heard I saying, Blessing, and honour, and glory, and power be unto Him that sitteth on the throne, and unto the Lamb, for ever and ever. And the four living creatures said, Amen. And the four and twenty elders fell down and worshipped Him that liveth for ever and ever' (chap. v. 11–14).

We here see with what intense fervour and devotion the Lamb, the Lord Jesus Christ, is worshipped in heaven. Would heavenly beings offer such worship—the same that is offered to Him upon the throne—to any other than a Divine personage? Would they be guilty of the idolatry of worshipping, after this manner, a creature like themselves?

Before dismissing these two chapters (iv.–v.), and entering on the prophetical part of the Revelation, it may be well to notice a few passages more particularly—

1. What are we to understand by 'the sea of glass, like unto crystal,' which John saw before the throne? (chap. iv. 6). Most commentators have supposed a reference here to 'the molten sea' which Solomon placed in the temple, intended for ablutions and purifications, which 'was ten cubits from one brim to the other.' But I doubt the fact of such a reference. The scenery in this vision is not that of the Jewish temple, but rather that of heaven itself, where was the throne of God, and the living creatures with the elders, and the countless myriads of angelic worshippers. I think that what seemed to the eye of the Apostle like a sea of polished crystal, was rather the *pavement* round about the throne, where the worshippers presented themselves. And this accords with another vision in this wonderful book, chap. xv., 'I saw as it were a sea of glass

mingled with fire; and they that have gotten the
victory over the beast, and over his image, and
over his mark, and over the number of his name,
stand on the sea of glass, with the harps of God.'
They do not bathe in the sea, or wash or purify
themselves in it. They need no ablutions in heaven.
But they *stand* upon it, as upon a polished and
glittering pavement.

2. Why is the song of redeeming mercy, sung by
the living creatures and the elders, here called a *new
song?* (chap. v. 9). Because, in the first place, it is
comparatively a new song in heaven. It has not
been sung there always, nor for a very long period.
Heaven had been inhabited by holy, happy creatures long ages before the new song had ever been
chanted in those blessed regions. Bright angels,
of different orders, had lifted up their hearts and
voices in praise to their Almighty Creator, saying,
'Thou art worthy, O Lord, to receive glory and
honour, for Thou hast created all things, and for
Thy pleasure they are, and they were created.'
But they had never sung the new song of redeeming mercy. They had no idea of such a song, and
no conception that it ever could or would be offered
up. The new song was sung on earth, before it
was heard in heaven. It was not till redeemed
souls had been gathered from the earth, and received up to heaven—that the living creatures

and the elders began to worship the Lamb, saying, 'Thou art worthy to open the book, and to loose the seals thereof, for Thou wast slain, and hast redeemed us unto God by Thy blood, out of every nation, and kindred, and tongue, and people.'

But this song may also be called new, on account of its *surpassing interest.* It is of such a nature that it will always be new. It can never grow old ; or (which is the same) become uninteresting. Redeeming love is of all subjects the most interesting in heaven. Of course, redeemed souls can never lose their interest in it ; while the angels are scarcely less engrossed in it than they. 'Into which things the angels desire to look.' Creative power, and sovereign wisdom, and preserving goodness, may lose, at length, something of their freshness and interest ; but not so redeeming grace. This subject will always be new ; for the riches of Christ are *unsearchable ;* and the love displayed in redemption *passeth knowledge ;* and the celebration of it in the songs of the blessed will never cease.

3. Near the close of the new song, the ransomed ones are represented as saying: 'Thou hast made us unto our God kings and priests, and *we shall reign upon the earth*' (chap. v. 10). What does this imply? Are the redeemed in heaven to come back to earth, and literally reign here with Christ? We think not. The whole scene presented in this vision is symboli-

cal.   The living creatures and the elders symbolize
the redeemed Church.   Their song implies, not that
they are literally to descend to earth, and have
crowns and kingdoms here, but that God's Church
is yet to reign upon the earth.   It is to predominate
over all other interests.   In the words of Daniel,
' The kingdom, and dominion, and greatness of the
kingdom under the whole heaven, shall be given to
the people of the saints of the Most High' (Daniel
vii. 27).

4. The grand chorus, in which all heaven unites,
is represented as closing thus : ' And every creature
which is in heaven, and on the earth, and under the
earth, and such as are in the sea, and all that are in
them, heard I saying, Blessing, and honour, and
glory, and power, be unto Him that sitteth on the
throne, and unto the Lamb, for ever and ever'
(chap. v. 13).

This language has often been quoted, as prov-
ing the doctrine of universal restoration.   ' However
long the reign of sin may be, the time will come
when every creature that is in heaven, or on earth,
or under the earth, or anywhere else, will be brought
to Christ, and unite in singing praises to God and
the Lamb for ever.'   It is a sufficient refutation of
this conceit to remember, that the language here
used is *not prophecy*.   It does not belong to the prophetical part of the Revelation.   That commences.

as I have said, with the opening of the sixth chapter. John is not predicting here a universal restoration to be accomplished far down in the cycles of time, but he is recording what he actually saw and heard at the time of the vision. And what did he see and hear? He heard every creature that was then in heaven—holy angels and the spirits of holy men—some of whose bodies were still mouldering on the earth, or under the earth, or in the sea—he heard them all singing with a loud voice, 'Blessing, and honour, and glory, and power, be unto Him that sitteth on the throne, and unto the Lamb, for ever and ever.' This is all the Universalism that this passage teaches; and it is, you see, no Universalism at all. All heaven was then occupied, and for ever will be, in singing songs of praise to God and the Lamb; while the beast and the false prophet are left to bite and gnaw their tongues for pain, and blaspheme the God of heaven, and still not repent of their evil deeds.

CHAPTER V.

THE OPENING OF THE SEALS.

REVELATION, CHAP. VI.

WE now come to the third, the prophetical part
of the Revelation—that relating to 'the
things which shall be hereafter.'

In fixing the date of this book, we excluded a
scheme of interpretation which refers most of these
prophecies to the death of Nero, and the destruction
of Jerusalem. They refer, undoubtedly, to leading
events in the history of God's Church, from the time
when they were written, to the end of the world.
Not that they furnish a syllabus, in minute detail,
of the civil and ecclesiastical history of the world;
nor is it likely that, in interpreting this book, we
are to follow throughout a chronological order.

Still there is certainly some regard paid to chro-
nology, for the book commences with the early
conquests of the Gospel, and ends with its final
triumph in this world, and its glorious consumma-
tion in heaven. But we are not to look for regular
chronological sequences from chapter to chapter,
nor anything like it. The visions and revelations
are mostly scenic, and great occurrences are repre-

sented frequently in successive scenes, that a more full and complete view of them may be exhibited.

The course of the Gospel through the ages, as set forth in these visions, is one, not of quiet prevalence, but rather of long and terrible conflict. Earth and hell are arrayed against it, and the contest is protracted and dreadful. The Church is represented as struggling against its mortal enemies —the dragon, the beast, and the false prophet—and is sometimes, apparently, on the verge of destruction. All the way, however, it is sustained by the ministry of angels, and by frequent manifestations of the Son of God; and in the end, the conflict comes out gloriously. The mystic Babylon is 'with violence thrown down, and shall be found no more at all.' 'The great whore, which did corrupt the earth with her fornications,' is brought to judgment, and is condemned. The beasts, which had so long ravaged the Church, are destroyed. The dragon, 'that old serpent, which is the devil and Satan,' is caught and imprisoned, to come out no more for a long period. A song of triumph goes up from all the host of heaven, saying, 'Alleluia! Salvation, and glory, and honour, and power, be unto the Lord our God; for true and righteous are His judgments!'

Such is, in brief, the plan of the Apocalypse; and the *object* of it—of Christ in revealing it, and of John in writing it—is very obvious. It was to instruct and warn the people of God. It was to strengthen and comfort them during their long conflict with earth and hell, setting before them its glorious termination, and the certainty of their final security and triumph. And who can tell how much the suffering children of God have been supported and comforted in view of these things? Confined in dark dungeons, and tortured in every form that a hellish ingenuity could invent; chained to the burning pile, or torn by savage beasts, or thrown from the tops of rocks, or drowned in the sea; who can tell how much they have been comforted by reflecting on the glowing visions of this wonderful book? It was here that they gathered arms for the deadly fight, and strength to triumph over their last enemy.

The revelations of the Apocalypse are imparted chiefly by means of *symbols*. And what are symbols? They are not the same as types, or figures of speech; but are rather the setting forth of moral ideas by pictures or natural objects. Thus, a circle is a symbol of eternity, having neither beginning nor end; an eye is a symbol of wisdom; a lion of courage; a lamb of meekness and gentleness; and a dove of innocence. Not a few of the symbols employed in the Revelation are interpreted either by the speaker or writer. Thus it is said in the first chapter: 'The seven stars are the angels of the seven Churches, and the seven candlesticks are the seven Churches.' And in the seventeenth chapter: 'The seven heads are seven mountains on which the woman sitteth;' and 'the ten horns are ten kings,' or kingdoms. So, in Daniel, 'The ram which thou sawest, having two horns, are the kings of Media and Persia; and the rough he-goat is the king of Grecia' (Dan. viii. 20.) And where the symbol is not explained, it is not usually of difficult interpretation. The nature of it will suggest its import, with at least sufficient clearness to answer the purpose of the writer. The design of prophecy does not require that there should be an explicit statement of what is to take place, with a detail of names, dates, and circumstances; but only such a statement as will show that some future event was intended, and will so far indicate or describe the event, that when it comes to pass, it may be seen that it really was the event referred to. It is no part of the object of the prophetic Scriptures to enable interpreters to prophesy, but rather to confirm their faith, and that of the whole Church, when the event shall actually have occurred. And this may be done by appropriate symbols, as well as in any other way.

It should be added, however, that peculiar care is necessary in the interpretation of symbols, lest the imagination get the better of sober judgment, and men retail,—as they often have done,—their own fancies in place of the truth of God.

But without further introduction, let us attempt the interpretation of some of the symbols in the chapter before us.

'And I saw, when the Lamb opened one of the seals; and I heard, as it were the noise of thunder, one of the four living creatures saying, Come and see. And I saw, and behold a white horse; and he that sat on him had a bow; and a crown was given unto him: and he went forth conquering, and to conquer' (Rev. vi. 1, 2).

The symbol here employed—a man, a conqueror, on a white horse—is interpreted in another part of the Revelation, 'I saw heaven opened, and behold a white horse; and He that sat on him was called Faithful and True; and in righteousness He doth judge and make war. His eyes were as a flame of fire, and on His head were many crowns; . . . and He was clothed with a vesture dipped in blood: and His name is called the Word (Logos) of God,' Rev. xix. 11–13. The symbol is the same as that in the chapter before us,—a triumphant conqueror on a white horse; and here we have His name in full—the Logos of God—the Lord Jesus Christ. It is Christ, therefore, who is here presented as 'going forth from conquering to conquer.'

The event predicted is, undoubtedly, the rapid

triumphs of the Gospel in the second and third centuries, immediately following the opening of the First Seal. In the first century, the Gospel spread into remote and distant places in every direction; still, it did not reach the people generally. 'It touched and glanced on every land,' but the interstices were not filled up; many places were left in darkness. In the next two centuries, this destitution was in a great measure remedied. The religion of Christ not only spread into regions before unoccupied, but it more deeply penetrated countries where it had already found its way. From the remotest east to the remotest west, and from the northern extremities of the Roman empire, and beyond them, far down into Ethiopia and Africa, we shall scarcely find a country in which the religion of Christ was not professed—Persia, Hither India, Mesopotamia, Armenia, Arabia, Asia Minor, Greece, Italy, Germany, Spain, Gaul, Britain, Egypt, and Northern Africa. Some of these countries were spread over with Churches and full of Christians; while in others, missionaries, private individuals, merchants, travellers, and in some instances captives, and even captive females, were busily at work, telling the story of a Saviour's death, and endeavouring to lead poor, blinded, groping, ruined sinners, into the way of life. It was impossible that Christianity, thus recommended and enforced, should

II

not prevail; and it did prevail. It triumphed over existing idolatries and superstitions, and soon reached a prodigious diffusion.

It was this fact which emboldened Tertullian to say, in his Apology: 'We are a people of yesterday; and yet we have filled every place belonging to you,—your cities, islands, castles, towns, assemblies, your very camp, your tribes, your companies, the palace, the forum, and the senate, leaving you nothing but your temples. You can count your armies, but our numbers, in some single provinces, are greater than they.'

Justin Martyr uses a similar language: 'There is no people, Greek or barbarian, or of any other race, by whatsoever appellation or manners they may be distinguished, however ignorant of arts or agriculture, whether they dwell in tents, or wander about in covered waggons, among whom prayers and thanksgivings are not offered in the name of the crucified Jesus, to the Father and Creator of all things.'

We have evidence that these statements are not exaggerations, from events which took place in the times of which we speak. During the reign of Trajan, the younger Pliny was governor of Bythinia; and so great was the number of Christians brought before him for trial and punishment, that he knew not what to do with them, and wrote to the emperor for advice. He had put many to death, on a profession of their faith; but the more accusers were encouraged, the more the victims were multiplied, until the numbers brought up for trial quite appalled him. To his request for instructions, the emperor replied: 'The Christians must not be sought after, nor must anonymous accusers be received. If any confess themselves to be Christians, and persist in it, let them be punished; but if any renounce their profession, and evince their sincerity by offering supplication to our gods, let them be pardoned.'

The same thing was acted over in the time of Adrian, when the proconsul of Asia wrote to him for advice. The priests stirred up the people at the public shows and games, to demand, with united voice, the destruction of the Christians; and these public clamours could not be safely disregarded. Whereupon the proconsul wrote to Adrian, that it seemed to him inhuman and unjust to immolate such multitudes of men and women, who had been convicted of no crime, just to gratify a furious mob. To this the emperor replied, as Trajan had done before him: 'The Christians shall not be disturbed without cause, nor shall sycophants be encouraged in their odious practices. If accusers will appear openly, and make charges against them, so as to give them an opportunity of answering for themselves, let them proceed in that manner, but not by rude demands and popular clamours.'

Facts such as these are more convincing than any private testimony as to the multitude of Christians at this time in the Roman provinces, and as to the general diffusion and triumph of the Gospel. They show that the great Redeemer had been riding forth from conquering to conquer, and had thus fully accomplished the prophetic import of the first seal which He had opened.

We come, then, to the Second Seal.

'And when He had opened the second seal, I heard the second living creature say, Come and see. And there went out another horse that was red; and power was given to him that sat thereon to take peace from the earth, and that they should kill one another: and there was given unto him a great sword' (Rev. vi. 3, 4).

The symbol here presented is obviously one of destruction by war. The horse is blood-red, and to him who sat on it was power given to take peace from the earth. A great sword was put into his hand, and those who before had been united in persecuting the people of God, were now to kill and destroy one another.

Such is the symbol: and we find its fulfilment near at hand. The reigns of Trajan and Adrian were both signalised by a mutual and terrible destruction of Jews and Romans—the first and greatest enemies of the Christians. Near the end of the reign of Trajan, the Jews in Egypt and Cyprus rebelled against the Roman government, and are reported to have put to death, with every mark of cruelty, four hundred and sixty thousand of their enemies. The Jews were speedily subdued by the Romans, and vast multitudes of them were slain. Eusebius, speaking of the rebellion, says: 'While the doctrine and Church of our Lord daily increased, the calamities of the Jews were aggravated by new miseries.'[1]

Shortly after this, in the reign of Adrian, the Jews were led into a new rebellion by one who pretended to be the Messiah. He was called Barchochebas, or *Son of the Star;* because he pretended to be the star foretold by Balaam (Num. xxiv. 17). The whole Jewish nation rose in arms against the Roman government, and murdered all who fell into their hands. But the rebellion, as before, was put down, and a terrible retribution was visited upon the Jews. They lost a thousand cities and fortresses, and 580,000 of their people perished. Adrian destroyed Jerusalem a second time, and built a new city in place of it, into which no Jew was permitted to enter.

Thus the original persecutors of the Christians,

[1] Ecc. Hist., Book iv. chap. 2.

according to the prediction, 'killed and destroyed *one another.*' The Romans, by their idolatries and cruelties, provoked the Jewish nation to rebellion; and, by following a false Messiah instead of the true, the Jews were brought to desolation. Thus, obviously and almost literally, were the indications of the second seal accomplished.

The Third Seal.

'And when he had opened the third seal, I heard the third living creature say, Come and see. And I beheld, and lo a black horse; and he that sat on him had a pair of balances in his hand. And I heard a voice in the midst of the four living creatures say, A measure of wheat for a penny, and three measures of barley for a penny; and see thou hurt not the oil and the wine' (Rev. vi. 5, 6).

The measure here spoken of was a *chœnix*,—an Attic measure, about equal to our quart. The penny was a *denarius*—the price of a day's labour—worth nearly fourteen cents. According to this, a day's labour would purchase only a quart of wheat, or three quarts of barley, indicating a great scarcity of bread. The injunction, too, to take care of the oil and the wine, the olives and vineyards, indicates a coming scarcity of these productions. In short, the entire symbol,—the black horse, the price of provisions, the man with his balances to weigh them out,—all wear a sombre aspect, and indicate a distressing scarcity of the necessaries of life.

Such is the symbol here presented; and when we look into the Roman history, we find it signally accomplished. A distressing scarcity prevailed in Italy and Rome during the reigns of the Antonines and their successors, to the time of Severus,—a period of nearly fifty years. Tertullian, who lived in these times, speaks of deluging rains and ruined harvests, bringing the utmost distress upon the people; which things he interprets as judgments upon them for persecuting the Christians.

In the reign of Antoninus Pius, Aurelius Victor says, that there was such a scarcity of provisions at Rome as to cause a tumult, in which the people were ready to stone the emperor. Julius Capitolinus speaks of the same thing, and adds: 'The emperor was fain to supply the scarcity of corn, wine, and oil, out of his own treasury.'

In the reign of his successor, Marcus Antoninus, we have a like account of scarcity, amounting almost to famine. Mr Echard[1] tells of the rise of the river Tiber, till it amounted to an inundation, overwhelming a considerable part of Rome. The flood bore along with it a multitude of people and of cattle, desolated the country, and caused a famine. This

[1] Roman History.

disaster was followed by earthquakes, the burning of cities, and an infinite number of ravenous insects, which darkened the air, and wasted what the floods had left.

In the next reign—that of Commodus—Dio tells us that 'there was such a scarcity of provisions, that the people rose and killed Cleander, the emperor's favourite.' This scarcity continued and increased during the wars and revolutions which followed, until the time of Severus. He made it one great object of his reign to remedy this standing evil, and provide against it in the future.

This protracted scarcity, of more than fifty years, was a striking fulfilment of the revelations of the third seal.

The Fourth Seal.

'And when he had opened the fourth seal, I heard the voice of the fourth living creature say, Come and see. And I looked, and behold a pale horse; and his name that sat on him was Death, and Hell followed with him: and power was given unto them over the fourth part of the earth, to kill with sword, and with hunger, and with death, and with the beasts of the earth' (Rev. vi. 7, 8).

The import of this frightful symbol can hardly be mistaken. Here was a 'pale horse,' with the image of Death seated upon him. Pale is a usual epithet of death—*pallidam mortem*, say the poets.

And Hell (hades) followed with it. Hades, in the Bible, signifies either the grave, or the place of future punishment of the wicked. It is never used in the Scriptures to signify the abode of the holy dead. It is the wicked, not the righteous, who are to be turned into *sheol* (*hades*) (Ps. ix. 17). 'And power was given unto them (death and hades) over the fourth part of the earth'—the Roman earth— 'to kill with the sword, with hunger, and with death,' *i.e.*, with pestilence, which is often used in Scripture as the synonym of death—'and with the beasts of the earth.' In the Hebrew prophets these are styled God's sore judgments. 'For thus saith the Lord; How much more when I send my *four sore judgments* upon Jerusalem, the sword, and the famine, and the noisome beast, and the pestilence, to cut off from it man and beast?' (Ezek. xiv. 21). The whole representation here is one of destruction and death, coming, not merely (as in the preceding seals) by famine and war, but also by pestilence, and the beasts of the earth. We shall see how the prediction was fulfilled.

Septimius Severus was on the throne at the commencement of the third century, and reigned till the year 211. During the next sixty years, the empire was in continual revolution and convulsion. There were not less than sixty aspirants to the throne, and more than twenty actually mounted it,—several

I

of whom, as Caracalla, Macrinus, Heliogabalus, and Maximin, were among the vilest of mankind. These intestine divisions gave courage to the enemies of Rome, particularly to the Persians and the northern barbarians, for it was at this period that we first hear of the Goths, as breaking into the dominions of Rome. Valerian too, a persecutor of the Christians, was taken prisoner by Sapor, king of Persia, and treated by him with great cruelty till his death.

Scarcity of provisions and famine, the usual effect of wars, and more especially civil wars, prevailed to an alarming extent. These things are mentioned by Dionysius of Alexandria, and by Cyprian, bishop of Carthage. ' After these things,' says Dionysius, speaking of the Decian persecution, ' wars and famine came upon us.' Cyprian, in his ' Apology for the Christians,' takes notice of the perpetual wars and famines of these times. These things were charged, as usual, upon the Christians. ' The gods are angry,' cried the priests, ' because their altars are forsaken; therefore has this distress come upon us.' Cyprian insists, on the contrary, that these great calamities, which had been before predicted, came upon the world, not because the Christians rejected the idolatrous Roman worship, but because the Romans rejected the worship of the true God, and persecuted His people.

The peculiar judgment indicated in the prediction before us, is *pestilence*,—the usual concomitant of famine and war. And this is specially mentioned by ancient historians. 'In the reigns of Gallus and Volusian,' says Zonoras, 'a plague infested the provinces. Beginning in Ethiopia, it spread itself through the whole east and west, destroyed the inhabitants of many cities, and continued for fifteen years.' Zosimus takes notice of the same calamity. ' While war raged in every part, a pestilence spread through the towns and villages, destroying the remnant of mankind. So great a destruction had never before happened.' Eutropius also says, 'that the reigns of Gallus and Volusian were only memorable for pestilence and grievous distempers.'

Of this unparalleled pestilence, Gibbon gives the following account: 'Famine is almost always followed by epidemical diseases, the effect of scanty and unwholesome food. Other causes must, however, have contributed to the furious plague which, from the year 250 to the year 265, raged without interruption in every province, every city, and almost every family in the Roman empire. During a part of this time five thousand persons died daily at Rome; and many towns that had escaped the hands of the barbarians were entirely depopulated.'[1]

Of the ravages of wild beasts during this melancholy period particular mention is made by Arno-

---

[1] Decline and Fall, vol. i. p. 150.

bius. Within a year after the death of Gallienus, they made their appearance in many provinces, and, like other evils, were charged upon the Christians, because they had roused the anger of the gods. Arnobius defends the Christians against this charge, by showing that ravenous beasts had prevailed in the previous ages, long before the date of Christianity.[1]

In the prediction before us, power was given to these several plagues over the fourth part of the Roman earth. Whether they actually prevailed to this extent, it is impossible to say. Mr Gibbon makes the proportion of those destroyed much greater than this. He goes into a calculation to show that, by the calamities which have been mentioned, not less than half of the inhabitants of the vast empire of Rome perished,—enough surely to answer to the symbol of 'Death upon the Pale Horse.'

The Fifth Seal.

' And when he had opened the fifth seal, I saw under the altar the souls of them that were slain for the word of God, and for the testimony which they held: and they cried with a loud voice, saying, How long, O Lord, holy and true, dost thou not judge and avenge our blood on them that dwell on the earth? And white robes were given unto every

[1] Disp. Adv. Gentes Libri, i. p. 5.

one of them; and it was said unto them, that they
should rest yet for a little season, until their fellow-
servants also and their brethren, that should be
killed as they were, should be fulfilled' (Rev. vi.
9–11).

There is some change of scene presented in this
symbol. Previously there had been a throne, and
He that sat upon it, surrounded by the elders and
the living creatures. But now there is a vision of
the temple in heaven, with its altars and other appur-
tenances. And this change may account for it, that
John no longer hears a voice from the living creatures, inviting him to come and see. At the foot of
one of the altars[1]—the place of prayer—John saw
the souls of the martyrs, 'who had been slain for the
word of God, and for the testimony which they
held;' and they were engaged in supplication:
'How long, O Lord, holy and true, dost thou not
judge and avenge our blood on them that dwell
on the earth?'

This does not imply that the martyrs in heaven
have any malice towards their former persecutors;
but they implore that the terrible scenes of torture and slaughter on the earth may cease, and
that God would magnify His glorious justice, in

---

[1] There were two altars in the temple,—the altar of burnt offerings,
where was presented the morning and evening sacrifice; and the altar
of incense. It is likely that the altar of incense is here referred to.

visiting upon the infamous destroyers of His people that punishment which they deserve. They implore that this may be done speedily. The answer to their prayer is, that they must forbear a little season. Others are waiting for the crown of martyrdom, and their destinies must be fulfilled. Meanwhile, the suppliants are invested with peculiar honours. White robes are given to every one of them; denoting that they are in the number of those 'who have washed their robes, and made them white in the blood of the Lamb.'

The import of this instructive symbol cannot be mistaken. It refers to the persecutions of the third and fourth centuries, and more especially to the last and most terrible of them—that under Diocletian.

At the commencement of the fourth century, the vast empire of Rome was governed by four rulers, viz., Diocletian and Maximian, with the title of Augustus; and Galerius and Constantius, with the title of Cæsar. The state of the Church was peaceful and happy. Christians were regarded with favour, and admitted to the most important civil offices; spacious buildings were erected for public worship, to which the people resorted without fear; and they had little more to hope for, unless it were that one or more of the emperors should embrace their religion. Under these circumstances, the pagan priests and populace began to be alarmed, lest the power which they had so long wielded should pass out of their hands. They first began to work upon the fears and prejudices of Diocletian, —who was an old man, and whom they knew to be both timid and credulous,—to induce him to persecute the Christians. But failing here, they next tried their arts upon Galerius, who was son-in-law to Diocletian; and with him they were more successful. He, being a cruel and fanatical pagan, persuaded Diocletian to publish an edict, requiring that the temples of the Christians should be demolished, their sacred books burned, and they deprived of all civil rights and honours. This decree did not aim directly at the *lives* of the Christians; and yet many, because they refused to give up their sacred books, were put to death.

Not long after the publication of this first edict, there were two conflagrations in the palace at Nicomedia, which were charged upon the Christians, and many of them were, by an imperial edict, put to the torture, with a view to extort confessions. Nearly at the same time there were insurrections in Armenia and Syria, which provoked the emperor to pass a third edict, committing all Christian bishops and ministers to prison, that, by tortures and punishments they might be compelled to offer sacrifice to the gods. In consequence of this order, the prisons, destined for the vilest criminals, were soon filled with bishops, presbyters, deacons, and other Church officers, many of whom were put to death, while others were exiled, or banished to the mines.

But the malice of Galerius was not yet satisfied. In the following year he induced Diocletian to pass his fourth and final edict, compelling all Christians to offer sacrifice to the gods under penalty of death.

The malice of the persecutors could go no further, and the condition of the Church, more especially in the eastern provinces, seemed to be hopeless. And what rendered it more so was, that Galerius, just at this time, succeeded in deposing Diocletian and Maximian, and thus became sole emperor of the East. His avowed purpose was to put an end to the Christian religion; and he set himself about it with the ferocity and ingenuity of a fiend.

It was not death which the Christians dreaded so much as the various and terrible tortures by which it was preceded. Mr Gibbon says: 'It would be easy to fill many pages with disgustful accounts of racks and scourges, of iron hooks and red-hot beds, and of other torments, which fire and steel, and savage beasts, and more savage men, could inflict on the human body.' Milner says: 'The prisons were full, and unheard of tortures were invented. Some were split down by axes; some were mutilated and cut in pieces; some had molten lead poured into their bodies; some were sawn asunder; while others were suspended, with the head downward, over a slow fire, till they were suffocated and consumed.'

I might pursue these hideous details to almost any length, but I need not. No wonder the souls of the martyrs, under the heavenly altar, were constrained to cry out, 'How long?' and to invoke the seemingly tardy justice of the Almighty to put a stop to such abominable deeds. Thus terribly were the portents of the fifth seal accomplished.

The Sixth Seal.

'And I beheld when He had opened the sixth seal, and, lo, there was a great earthquake; and the sun became black as sackcloth of hair, and the moon became as blood; and the stars of heaven fell unto the earth, even as a fig-tree casteth her untimely figs, when she is shaken of a mighty wind. And the heaven departed as a scroll when it is rolled together; and every mountain and island were moved out of their places. And the kings of the earth, and the great men, and the rich men, and the chief captains, and the mighty men, and every bondman, and every free man, hid themselves in the dens and in the rocks of the mountains; and said to the mountains and rocks, Fall on us, and hide us from the face of Him that sitteth on the throne, and from

K

the wrath of the Lamb: for the great day of His
wrath is come, and who shall be able to stand?'
(Rev. vi. 12–17).

The events here described were all seen in pano-
ramic vision. They were pictured on that roll of a
book which the Lamb took out of the hand of Him
that sat upon the throne, and were exhibited, as
they could be, upon the breaking of the sixth seal.
They are all of them symbolical; nor are the symbols of difficult interpretation. The earthquake
denotes a great shaking of the religious and political earth—a mighty change—a stupendous revolution. The darkening of the sun and moon, and the
falling of the stars, set forth the overturning of
thrones, and the downfall of rulers and dignitaries.
The departure of the visible heavens, like the rolling
up of a scroll of parchment, and the moving of the
mountains and islands out of their places, are all a
part of the same mighty change. The luminaries
which had before studded the political heavens are
no longer there. They are rolled together, and put
out of sight, and potentates and powers, which had
seemed like the fastnesses of the earth, have passed
away.

The phraseology here used may seem strange to
modern ears, but it is in strict accordance with the prophetic language of the Old Testament. Thus Isaiah,
predicting the downfall of idolatrous kingdoms,

says: 'The stars of heaven and the constellations thereof shall not give their light: the sun shall be darkened in his going forth, and the moon shall not cause her light to shine. And I will punish the world for their evil, and the wicked for their iniquity' (Isa. xiii. 10). 'The host of heaven shall be dissolved, and the heavens shall be rolled together as a scroll: and all their host shall fall down, as the leaf falleth from off the vine, and as a falling fig from the fig-tree' (Isa. xxxiv. 4).

Our Saviour uses similar language in predicting the destruction of Jerusalem: 'The sun shall be darkened, and the moon shall not give her light, and the stars shall fall from heaven, and the powers of the heavens shall be shaken' (Matt. xxiv. 29).

The concluding verses under the sixth seal set forth the terror and affright which the revolution thus predicted shall occasion. The great ones of the earth, with all its guilty inhabitants, shall flee and hide themselves in the dens, and in the rocks of the mountains, and shall say to the mountains, 'Fall on us, and hide us from the face of Him who sitteth on the throne, and from the wrath of the Lamb.'

The mighty revolution here symbolically portrayed is, without doubt, the revolution under Constantine, which took place immediately upon the close of the Diocletian persecution. Upon the death of Constantius Chlorus, who, with the title of Cæsar, governed the western provinces of the empire, and who, though a pagan, had not participated in the recent persecutions, his son Constantine was, by the army, proclaimed his successor. He had several colleagues and rivals, all of whom sought his life ; but, one after another, they were taken out of the way. Maxentius and Licinius he vanquished in battle ; Maximin committed suicide ; while Galerius, the chief instigator of the late persecution, was smitten with an incurable disease, attended by such insupportable torments, that he often attempted to destroy himself, but was prevented. Thus the political sun and moon of Rome were darkened, and the stars fell to the earth.

Constantine became sole emperor of Rome in the year 323. Previous to this, he had become a decided believer in the Christian religion. He soon effected an entire revolution in the civil and religious state of the empire. In place of the Roman eagle, he carried before his armies a representation of the cross. He removed the seat of empire from Rome to Constantinople, and adopted a new form of government, putting the administration of it into the hands of four principal officers, called Prætorian Prefects. The great lights of the heathen world— the powers civil and religious—were all eclipsed and obscured ; heathen augurs and soothsayers were suppressed; heathen priests and magistrates were removed; heathen temples were demolished, and their revenues appropriated to better uses. In short, a new religion was established, and a new order of things arose in the world's history. Paganism was effectually overthrown, its votaries, with their idols, were cast to the moles and the bats; and, after lingering for a little time, it passed finally away. Here, surely, was change enough accomplished to be indicated by the sublime and awful imagery of the sixth seal.

CHAPTER VI.

THE FIRST FOUR TRUMPETS.
REVELATION, CHAPS. VII., VIII.

' AND after these things I saw four angels standing on the four corners of the earth, holding the four winds of the earth, that the wind should not blow on the earth, nor on the sea, nor any tree. And I saw another angel ascending from the east, having the seal of the living God: and he cried with a loud voice to the four angels, to whom it was given to hurt the earth and the sea, saying, Hurt not the earth, neither the sea, nor the trees, till we have sealed the servants of our God in their foreheads. And I heard the number of them which were sealed: an hundred and forty-four thousand of all the tribes of the children of Israel'—(*i.e.,* twelve thousand from each of the twelve tribes) (Rev. vii. 1–8).

The seventh chapter of the Revelation may be regarded as an appropriate conclusion of the events predicted under the sixth seal. ' After these things' (*i.e.,* the revolution which has been described), John sees four angels standing on the four corners of the earth, holding the four winds of heaven, that, for a time, they should not blow on the earth, nor on the sea, nor on any tree. Winds, in the language of the prophets, are the appropriate symbols of commotions and wars. Thus Jeremiah, speaking of the overthrow of the Persians, says: 'And upon Elam will I bring the four winds from the four quarters of heaven, and will scatter them toward all those winds; and there shall be no nation whither the outcasts of Elam shall not come' (Jer. xlix. 36). The restraining of the four winds, therefore, indicates, that commotions and wars should be temporarily restrained in the Roman earth, and that the revolution before predicted should be followed by a season of peace.

And so, in fact, it was. When Constantine had triumphed over all his enemies, and become firmly seated on his throne, there was a season of unusual tranquillity. There were few or no wars or civil commotions to the end of his reign. On this subject Eusebius speaks earnestly and particularly, applying the language of the Psalmist to his own times: 'Come hither, and behold the works of the Lord, what wonders He hath wrought in the earth. He maketh wars to cease unto the ends of the earth; he breaketh the bow, and cutteth the spear asunder; he burneth the chariot in the fire.'[1] Lactantius also tells us, in

---

[1] Ps. xlvi. 8, 9, according to the Septuagint.

the same triumphant strain, that 'tranquillity being restored throughout the earth, the Church, which was lately ruined, riseth again. Now, after the agitations of so great a tempest, a calm air and the desired light became resplendent. Now hath God relieved the afflicted, and wiped away the tears of the sorrowful.' These are testimonies of contemporary Christian writers. Some medals of Constantine are still preserved, with the head of the emperor on one side, and this inscription on the other,— BEATA TRANQUILLITAS—Blessed tranquillity.

It was during this time of tranquillity that the servants of God were to be sealed in their foreheads, —an allusion to the ancient custom of marking servants in their foreheads, to show who they were, and to whom they belonged.

We are not to understand that any visible mark was at this time put upon the foreheads of Christians. But God goes forth, by His providence and grace, to search out His people, and sanctify and seal them for himself. The phraseology implies that a *selection* is to be made. All are not sealed who bear the Christian name, and are able to make a fair show in the flesh ; but God seeks out His own, and puts a mark upon them, that henceforth He may know, and the world may know, to whom they belong. They bear unmistakably ' the spot of His children.'

This sealing process was exceedingly appropriate in the times of which we speak. Christianity was undergoing a new trial. It had borne the brunt of severe and protracted persecution. Can it bear as well the trial of great prosperity? Christianity was now the religion of the court and the state. It was exceedingly popular; and multitudes were eager to make a profession of it. Thousands and thousands crowded into the Churches, and solicited baptism. It is said that twelve thousand men were baptized at Rome in a single year, besides a proportionate number of women and children.

Nor were the guardians of the Churches as particular as they should have been in looking into the character of those who were admitted. The consequence was, that the Churches were rapidly filling up with mere worldly members,—ambitious, selfish, ostentatious, proud,—who sought its fellowship only that they might secure their worldly ends. Such were the characters, in many instances, of the bishops and ministers. It is obvious, therefore, that the Church needed a sifting. A messenger of mercy must pass through it, and separate, so far as possible, the precious from the vile. He must search out and seal those who belong to Christ. He must prepare the wheat for the heavenly garner, and leave the chaff to the winds. In no other way can the Church of God be prepared for those ages of darkness and

L

conflict through which it has yet to pass, and for those triumphs and glories which await it in the distant future, on earth and in heaven.

The sealing process was of the first importance at this very time. And John tells us the number that were sealed,—a small number, it would seem, in comparison with the whole—a definite number, in place of an indefinite. There were sealed a hundred and forty-four thousand out of the several tribes of Israel.

The word Israel is here used, as it often is in the Scriptures, in a symbolical sense. It stands for the Church in general—the whole Israel of God. This, whether made up of Jews or Gentiles, is the Israel here spoken of, from among whom the sealed ones are selected and taken.

When the sealing process was over, a new vision presented itself to the view of the apostle: 'I beheld, and, lo, a great multitude, which no man could number, of all nations, and kindreds, and people, and tongues, stood before the throne, and before the Lamb, clothed with white robes, and palms in their hands; and cried with a loud voice, saying, Salvation to our God which sitteth upon the throne, and unto the Lamb' (Rev. vii. 9, 10).

This part of the service belonged exclusively to the ransomed ones—those who had been redeemed from the earth. These, as being more

particularly interested, were permitted to lead off
in the heavenly anthem. But when their part was
performed, '*all the angels* stood round about the
throne, and about the elders and the four living
creatures, and fell before the throne on their faces,
and worshipped God, saying, Amen: Blessing, and
glory, and wisdom, and thanksgiving, and honour,
and power, and might, be unto our God for ever
and ever. Amen' (Rev. vii. 11, 12).

The vision was a heavenly one, and this is one
of those songs of triumph,—of which there are
several in the book of Revelation,—which are
sung by the heavenly choirs, in view of the victories of Christ's cause upon the earth; thus showing the sympathy of heaven with earth, and the
deep interest which is felt above in all that concerns
the militant Church below.

Among the crowd of ransomed worshippers about
the throne, John saw some whose robes were very
white, and who seemed to be invested with peculiar
honours; and he was anxious to know who these
were, and whence they came. And one of the
elders answered and said, 'These are they which
came out of great tribulation, and have washed their
robes, and made them white in the blood of the
Lamb' (Rev. vii. 14). The reference here is, without doubt, *primarily*, to the martyrs who had come
out of the late persecution; but, *ultimately*, to all

those who are called to great sufferings in the cause of Christ, who bear them meekly, and triumph over them. To all such, the closing words of comfort and promise may be regarded as addressed: 'They shall hunger no more, neither thirst any more; neither shall the sun light on them, nor any heat. For the Lamb which is in the midst of the throne shall feed them, and shall lead them unto living fountains of waters: and God shall wipe away all tears from their eyes' (Rev. vii. 16, 17).

The way is now prepared for the opening of the Seventh Seal, the revelations of which are of great extent, including the seven succeeding trumpets, and reaching down to the millennium.

'And when he had opened the seventh seal, there was silence in heaven about the space of half an hour. And I saw the seven angels which stood before God; and to them were given seven trumpets. And another angel came and stood at the altar, having a golden censer; and there was given unto him much incense, that he should offer it with the prayers of all saints upon the golden altar which was before the throne. And the smoke of the incense, which came with the prayers of the saints, ascended up before God out of the angel's hand. And the angel took the censer, and filled it with fire of the altar, and cast it into the earth: and there were voices, and thunderings, and lightnings, and an earthquake' (Rev. viii. 1–5).

Upon the opening of the seal, seven angels are seen standing before the throne, to whom are given seven trumpets,—the signals of alarm and war. But before going forth on this mission of blood, there is a half hour's silence in heaven, and a season of devout worship, the imagery of which is taken from the Jewish temple. In performing the service of the temple, one of the priests entered daily into the holy place, and, with his censer filled with coals from the altar of burnt-offering, approached the altar of incense, and burned incense before the Lord. The incense was a symbol of prayer; and, while it was burning, the people were silently offering up their prayers. They ' were praying without at the time of incense.' Thus Zechariah was employed when Gabriel appeared to him, and promised him a son (Luke i. 9, 10).

A similar service seemed now to be performing in heaven. An ' angel came and stood at the altar, having a golden censer; and much incense given unto him, that he should offer it with the prayers of all saints upon the golden altar which was before the throne.' While this service was in progress, there was, of course, silence in heaven for the space of half an hour. Perhaps this scene was designed to denote that great evils were impending, and that earth and heaven should unite their supplications, that they might, if possible, be averted or mitigated. But the intercessions offered do not prevail. The causes of the coming inflictions lie too deep to be removed by prayer. And so the interceding angel casts his censer to the earth, and 'there are voices, and thunderings, and lightnings, and an earthquake,' —indicating new commotions and great calamities to be speedily inflicted.

'And the seven angels which had the seven trumpets prepared themselves to sound' (Rev. viii. 6).

The First Trumpet.

'The first angel sounded, and there followed hail and fire mingled with blood, and they were cast upon the earth: and the third part of trees was burnt up, and all green grass was burnt up' (Rev. viii. 7).

I agree with those interpreters who regard the blast of the first four of these trumpets as indicating the calamities, which fell upon the western Roman empire, and resulted in its overthrow in the latter part of the fifth century. History marks four of these incursions—the sweeping of the fiery storm— which followed each other in rapid succession, and which left behind them naught of that mighty power which had so long ruled at Rome, except the name.

The symbols employed under the first trumpet,—

' hail and fire mingled with blood,'—indicate a great and sweeping destruction, which seems to have been fulfilled in the invasion of Alaric, king of the Goths, in the year 410.

Alaric had been employed under Theodosius, and in his armies had acquired a knowledge of the art of war. Upon the death of Theodosius, he was disappointed in not being raised to the head of the Roman armies, and so he revolted, and became a leader of the Goths. He first invaded and conquered Greece, destroying the males who were of an age to bear arms, and driving away the females, with the spoil and cattle of the flaming villages. He next determined to enter Italy; and to plant, if possible, the Gothic standard on the walls of Rome. He was checked in his first attempt by the army of Stilicho; but he soon returned, swept over the country, and more than once besieged and pillaged the imperial city. The sufferings at Rome in these sieges were beyond description. In repeated instances, mothers were compelled to cook and eat their own children. Meanwhile, the imbecile emperor Honorius and his court had concealed themselves in the fastnesses of Ravenna.

From Italy, Alaric proceeded to invade the cities and fertile provinces of Gaul. The flourishing city of Metz was surprised and destroyed, and many thousands of Christians were massacred in the

church. Worms was taken after a long and ob-
stinate siege. Strasburg, Spires, Rheims, Tournay,
Arras, and Amiens, experienced the cruel oppression
of the Gothic yoke; and the flames of war spread
from the banks of the Rhine over the greatest part
of the seventeen provinces of Gaul. That rich and
extensive country, from the ocean to the Pyrénées
and the Alps, was delivered to the barbarians, who
drove before them, in a promiscuous crowd, the
people of all classes, with the spoils of their houses,
their fields, and their altars.

It would be unsafe to say that precisely a third
part of the western Roman empire was over-run and
pillaged by Alaric; but enough of it fell under his
destroying hand to justify the prophetical indications of the first trumpet.

The Second Trumpet.

' And the second angel sounded, and as it were
a great mountain burning with fire was cast into the
sea: and the third part of the sea became blood;
and the third part of the creatures which were in
the sea, and had life, died; and the third part of the
ships were destroyed' (Rev. viii. 8, 9).

The symbols here indicate some great and angry
power, like a burning mountain, precipitated upon
the maritime parts of the Roman empire, by which
its cities would be wasted and its commerce destroyed. If we were correct in our interpretation

of the previous trumpet, this must refer to Genseric and his ruthless Vandals. This invasion followed quick upon that of Alaric, commencing about the year 428, and continuing for the next forty years. The Goths and Vandals are usually mentioned together, and they seem to have been originally one people. They invaded the Roman empire together in the time of Theodosius. At a later period, the Vandals, under Genseric, passed through the whole of what is now France and Spain, and crossed over into Africa. They conquered Carthage, established an independent government, and thence through a long period ravaged the neighbouring coasts and islands, destroyed the ships and commerce of the Romans, and in this way hastened the downfall of the empire. The ambition of Genseric was without scruple and without bounds. In a little time, all the fruitful provinces lying between Tangier and Tripoli were overwhelmed. Where these marauders encountered resistance, they seldom gave quarter, and the death of their warriors was expiated by the ruin of the cities under whose walls they fell. The result of this invasion was the conquest of all Northern Africa, and the establishment of a power which waged perpetual war with Rome.

Genseric now resolved to establish a naval power; and to resolve and to execute were with him almost the same. His fleets soon claimed the empire of the Mediterranean, and his conquests provoked the sluggish emperor to oppose him. He, too, prepared a fleet; but at the first onset it fell into the hands of the Vandals, and they soon cast anchor at the mouth of the Tiber. Great Rome could offer no effectual resistance. The city was taken and given up to pillage and slaughter for fourteen successive days and nights.

Genseric continued his naval depredations to an advanced period of life. He repeatedly visited the coasts of Spain, Liguria, Tuscany, Campania, Apulia, Calabria, Dalmatia, Venice, Epirus, Sicily, and Greece, spreading terror and desolation from the pillars of Hercules to the Nile. As these freebooters were more desirous of spoil than of glory, they seldom attacked fortified cities, or engaged regular troops in the open field, but ravaged defenceless coasts and islands, carrying dismay and desolation wherever they appeared.

How far this description agrees with the symbols in the passage before us,—' a great mountain burning with fire cast into the sea,' by which a third part of the ships and the creatures in the sea were destroyed, I must leave to my readers to judge. If the career of Genseric and his Vandals were to be portrayed at all by symbols, I can hardly think of any symbols more appropriate than those presented under the second trumpet.

The Third Trumpet.

'And the third angel sounded, and there fell a great star from heaven, burning as it were a lamp, and it fell upon the third part of the rivers, and upon the fountains of waters; and the name of the star is called Wormwood: and the third part of the waters became wormwood; and many men died of the waters, because they were made bitter' (Rev. viii. 10, 11).

A star, in the language of the prophets, denotes some illustrious, distinguished personage,—sometimes a religious teacher, but more frequently a monarch, or some remarkable civil or military leader. Thus the fallen king of Babylon is called Lucifer, or the morning star. 'How art thou fallen from heaven, O Lucifer, son of the morning! how art thou cast down to the ground, which didst weaken the nations!' (Isa. xiv. 12). The star falling from heaven, or the blazing meteor gleaming through the sky, in the passage before us, may well denote some great military chieftain; and the result of his fall, turning every thing he touches into wormwood, shows him to be a most bitter enemy.

Following the train of thought which has been pursued thus far, considering the blasts of these trumpets as pre-figuring the personages and events which prepared the way for the downfall of the western Roman empire, we cannot be mistaken in supposing Attila, the leader of the terrible bands of Huns (who styled himself, and was styled by others, the 'Scourge of God'), as designated by the falling star.

After Alaric and Genseric, Attila occupies the next place among the destroyers of ancient Rome. It is true, indeed, that he was contemporary with Genseric, and died before him; but he commenced his ravages at a later period, and on this account may be regarded as coming after him. He came suddenly from the East, like a flaming meteor, gathering up in his progress an army of Huns, and pouring them down upon the more defenceless parts of the Roman empire. The portions of the empire most affected by the ravages of the Huns were precisely those designated by the blast of the third trumpet, viz.: 'the rivers and fountains of waters.' His depredations were chiefly confined to the sides of the Alps, those places whence the rivers flow down into Italy.

Attila was defeated in the battle of Chalons; but he soon recovered his vigour, collected his forces, and was prepared for another descent upon Italy. He destroyed Aquileia, and in his march from thence, the cities of Altinum, Concordia, and Padua, were reduced to ashes. He next spread himself over the fertile plains of Lombardy,—a land of rivers and streams, divided by the Po, and lying between the

Alps and Apennines. It was a saying worthy of the ferocious pride of Attila, that 'the grass never grew where his horse had trod.' At least a third part of the empire was invaded and desolated in his savage marches; and the result of his invasion was as disastrous as if a bitter star had fallen into all the rivers and fountains, and turned them into gall and wormwood.

The Fourth Trumpet.

'And the fourth angel sounded, and the third part of the sun was smitten, and the third part of the moon, and the third part of the stars; so as the third part of them was darkened, and the day shone not for a third part of it, and the night likewise' (Rev. viii. 12).

At the sounding of the fourth trumpet, the great lights of the Roman empire were eclipsed and darkened, so that they shone not clearly, and but for a part of the time. Genseric and Attila left the empire in a weak, impoverished, and desperate condition. It struggled on, however, through eight short and turbulent reigns, for the space of about twenty years, when it came to an end in the year 476. The last reigning emperor was Momyllus, —contemptuously called Augustulus, or the little Augustus. This change was effected by Odoacer, a Gothic chieftain, who, coming to Rome with an army, stripped Momyllus of his imperial robes, put an end to his dominion, and caused himself to be proclaimed king of Italy. He did not, however, change entirely the ancient form of government. If the sun was eclipsed, some of the lesser lights were allowed to remain. He still permitted the Romans to have their senate, their consuls, and other magistrates, and public affairs were transacted much as they had been in former days.

Odoacer reigned sixteen years, when his kingdom was overthrown by Theodoric, king of the Ostrogoths. The government was in his hands and in those of his successors, for the next sixty years.

CHAPTER VII.

THE FIFTH AND SIXTH TRUMPETS.

REVELATION, CHAP. IX.

I HAVE thus endeavoured to give the import of the four first trumpets, embracing the four successive blows which were struck upon western Rome by Alaric, Genseric, Attila, and Odoacer, until the empire fell to rise no more.

And now there is a pause between the sounding of the fourth trumpet and the fifth; a note of solemn, awful warning is heard from the heavens:

'And I beheld, and heard an angel flying through the midst of heaven, saying with a loud voice, Woe, woe, woe, to the inhabitants of the earth by reason of the other voices of the trumpet of the three angels, which are yet to sound!' (Rev. viii. 13).

The woe is repeated three times to show the certainty and intensity of it, and to call attention to what remains of this magnificent prophecy.

The Fifth Trumpet.

'And the fifth angel sounded, and I saw a star fall from heaven unto the earth: and to him was given the key of the bottomless pit. And he opened the bottomless pit; and there arose a smoke out of the pit, as the smoke of a great furnace; and the sun and the air were darkened by reason of the smoke of the pit. And there came out of the smoke locusts upon the earth: and unto them was given power, as the scorpions of the earth have power. And it was commanded them that they should not hurt the grass of the earth, neither any green thing, neither any tree; but only those men which have not the seal of God in their foreheads. And to them it was given that they should not kill them, but that they should be tormented five months; and their torment was as the torment of a scorpion, when he striketh a man. And in those days shall men seek death, and shall not find it; and shall desire to die, and death shall flee from them. And the shapes of the locusts were like unto horses prepared unto battle; and on their heads were as it were crowns like gold, and their faces were as the faces of men. And they had hair as the hair of women, and their teeth were as the teeth of lions. And they had breastplates, as it were breastplates of iron; and the sound of their wings was as the sound of chariots of many horses running to battle. And they had tails like unto scorpions, and there were stings in their tails; and their power was to hurt men five months. And they had a king over them, which is the angel of the bottomless pit, whose name in the Hebrew tongue is Abaddon, but in the Greek tongue hath his name Apollyon' (Rev. ix. 1–11).

I have said already that the four first trumpets foreshow the events which led to the downfall of the western Roman empire, which took place in the year 476. I agree with the most distinguished Protestant commentators, that the fifth and sixth trumpets relate to the Eastern empire, and to events which resulted in its overthrow.

The star which John saw fall from heaven on the sounding of the fifth trumpet denotes, as usual, a leader,—it may be a distinguished teacher, or a military chieftain, or both. It represents, in this case, I cannot doubt, Mohammed. He has the key of the bottomless pit, and opens it, and from it issues a smoke which darkens the whole atmosphere. With the smoke, there came forth also a prodigious army of locusts. A full description of the locusts is given, which shows that they were not literal locusts, but represent a mighty army—Mohammed's army of Saracen warriors. The fact that locusts were the selected symbols here, shows that the prophecy has an oriental application. Locusts are the periodical scourges of the east.

This army is commissioned, not to hurt the earth, or any green thing, but only the men that

N

have not the seal of God on their foreheads; referring back to the sealing spoken of in the seventh chapter. In other words, their commission is against, not God's sealed, sanctified ones, but the wicked of the earth—idolators, blasphemers, and apostate Christians. Nor were they to aim at destroying the lives even of these, but were to torment them for the space of five months.

But what are we to understand by these five months? Are they literal months, or do they denote a much longer period? It is insisted by some interpreters that they must be literal months, since the ravages of locusts are usually limited to the five warmest months of the year. But then these are not literal locusts—from the very description they cannot be—and hence the impropriety of limiting their ravages and torments to the short period of five literal months.

It is insisted by another class of interpreters that, in prophetic language, a day often stands for a year; and if so interpreted in this place, the ravages of the army denoted by the locusts would continue a hundred and fifty years.

With regard to this question of time, I remark that, in prophetic language, a day is often—not always—reckoned for a year. So it has been in other ages; so it may be here. Thus when it was predicted of the Israelites that they should wander in the wilderness forty years, it was added: 'After the number of the days in which ye searched the land, even forty days, *each day for a year*, shall ye bear your iniquities, even *forty years*' (Numb. xiv. 34). So the prophet Ezekiel, when predicting the siege and capture of Jerusalem, was directed to 'lie on his right side, and bear the iniquity of the house of Judah forty days; I have appointed thee *each day for a year*' (Ezek. iv. 6).

In the prophecy of Daniel, this mode of prophetic expression is unquestionably resorted to: 'Seventy weeks are determined upon thy people, and upon thy holy city, to finish the transgression, and to make an end of sins, and to make reconciliation for iniquity, and to bring in everlasting righteousness, and to seal up the vision and prophecy, and to anoint the Most Holy' (Dan. ix. 24). This prediction refers, undoubtedly, to the Messiah, and to the time when He should appear to make expiation for sin. The commencement of the seventy weeks is fixed by Daniel himself, or rather by the revealing angel. It was 'from the going forth of the decree to restore and to build Jerusalem' (Dan. ix. 25). The decree to restore and to build Jerusalem was given to Nehemiah, by Artaxerxes Longimanus, in the twentieth year of his reign (Neh. ii. 1). And from this time to the death of Christ, according to the best chronologists, is four hundred and ninety years—seventy weeks, counting a day for a year.

It is objected to this interpretation, that what our translators render 'seventy weeks,' is in the original of Daniel 'seventy seven,' which may mean seventy *sevens* of *years*, that is, four hundred and ninety years; thus bringing us to the same result, without supposing a day to stand for a year.

The only question here is; did Daniel, or the revealing angel, intend, by the seventy sevens, *sevens* of *days*, or *sevens* of *years?* We think he must have intended sevens of days, since, from the creation, time had been divided into weeks of seven days; so that a seven or sevens would naturally be understood to mean seven days, whether the word days was expressed or not. And critics have no reason or authority for changing the meaning into sevens of years, more than for changing it into sevens of months, or sevens of hours. A seven is naturally understood to be a *hebdomad*, a week o seven days. And so the word always has been understood and translated.[1] The proper translation of the passage before us is, therefore, that contained in our Bible: 'Seventy weeks are determined

[1] See not only the passages in Dan. ix. 24-26, but also in Dan. x. 2, 3; Ex. xxiv. 22; Numb. xxviii. 26; Deut. xvi. 9-16; 2 Chron. viii. 13; Jer. v. 24; Ezek. xlv. 21, etc.

upon thy people, and upon the holy city,' that is, seventy times seven days — four hundred and ninety days; and the fulfilment of the prophecy shows that each of these days must stand for a year.

There are other passages in Daniel in which the same mode of reckoning occurs, to which I shall refer in another connection. Instances of it also occur in the Revelation. It is said to the Church in Smyrna: 'The devil shall cast some of you into prison, that ye may be tried; and ye shall have tribulation ten days' (Rev. ii. 10). No one can suppose that the persecution here referred to would be limited to ten literal days. The reference is, undoubtedly, to the Diocletian persecution, which lasted ten years.

There are other instances in the Revelation in which the same notation of prophetic time is employed, particularly those in which 'the holy city is to be trodden under foot forty and two months;' and the two witnesses are to 'prophesy a thousand and two hundred and three score days;' and the mystical woman is to be nourished in the wilderness 'for a time and times and half a time;' and in which 'power was given unto the beast to continue forty and two months.[1] These notes of time, as I shall show, all refer to the same period, twelve

[1] See Rev. ii. 2, 3, and xii. 14, and xiii. 5.

hundred and sixty days, and stand for twelve hundred and sixty years, a day being reckoned for a year.[1]

If it be inquired, how we are to determine, in any given case, whether the days are to be understood literally, or otherwise, I answer, we are to be guided chiefly, as in other cases, by the connection and the sense. Thus, when it is said in Jeremiah: 'These nations shall serve the king of Babylon seventy years,' the connection shows that literal years are intended. But when Daniel predicts, in a passage already considered, the death of the Messiah at the end of seventy weeks, both the connection and the fulfilment show that a much longer period is indicated.

---

[1] Professor Cowles denounces 'this day-for-a-year theory as utterly baseless and false, and of course mischievous and delusive ;' and yet, strange to say, he does not himself interpret the notation of time in the Apocalypse literally, but prolongs them indefinitely, or as much as he has occasion. Thus, it is said expressly of the two witnesses, that they prophesied twelve hundred and sixty days. But Professor Cowles says, 'It matters not how long the two witnesses did actually testify to the Jews before the fall of their city,' p. 127. They must have testified, according to his theory, at least forty years, for he reckons John the Baptist to be the first of them, p. 132. So the mystical woman is protected in the wilderness 'for a time, times, and half a time,' or three years and a half. But according to Professor Cowles, 'We have no occasion to inquire for the same historic duration of either the Church's protection or of her persecution. God kept her in the wilderness *as long as the occasion demanded,*' p. 147. So the forty and two months of the beast's continuance indicates, according to Professor Cowles, 'an indefinite period of calamity,' p. 155. And even the thousand years of the millennium does not, in his reckoning, signify a thousand years, but a vastly longer period.

But to return from this indispensable digression to the case of the Saracen warriors, whose ravages were to continue five months, every one must see that five literal months cannot be here intended. A much longer period must be indicated. In the language of prophecy,—such as we have seen is often used,—these five months, or one hundred and fifty days, may stand for one hundred and fifty years. Let us inquire, then, whether the depredations and conquests of the Saracens continued as long as this.

The Saracens first issued from the desert into Syria, and commenced their wars upon Christian nations about the year 629. From this time, for the next hundred and fifty years, they were the most successful warriors on the earth. They carried their conquests through Egypt and all northern Africa, and then through the greater part of Spain and into France. At the same time, they twice besieged Constantinople, and laid waste the greater part of the eastern Roman empire. They entered Europe from the East, intending and expecting to unite their eastern and western conquests somewhere in Italy, and to have all Christendom at their feet. But they were defeated and driven back in France by Charles Martel, in the year 732. Soon after this, their conquests were checked in the East; and by the year 779—one hundred and fifty

years from the commencement of their ravages —
their power to injure had, in great measure, ceased.
The caliphs had become rich, luxurious, and effemi-
nate; they built cities, palaces, and castles; they
devoted much time to the pursuits of science and
the arts of peace.   They did not cease to exist as a
people, but their power to do hurt was taken away.
They were no longer a terror to their Christian
neighbours, and to the nations of the earth.

'One woe is past; and, behold, there come two
woes more hereafter' (Rev. ix. 12).

The Sixth Trumpet.

'And the sixth angel sounded, and I heard a
voice from the four horns of the golden altar which
is before God, saying to the sixth angel which
had the trumpet, Loose the four angels which
are bound in the great river Euphrates.   And the
four angels were loosed, which were prepared for
an hour, and a day, and a month, and a year, for to
slay the third part of men.   And the number of the
army of the horsemen were two hundred thousand
thousand: and I heard the number of them.   And
thus I saw the horses in the vision, and them that
sat on them, having breastplates of fire, and of
jacinth, and brimstone : and the heads of the
horses were as the heads of lions; and out of their
mouths issued fire and smoke and brimstone.   By
these three was the third part of men killed, by the

fire, and by the smoke, and by the brimstone, which issued out of their mouths. For their power is in their mouth, and in their tails; for their tails were like unto serpents, and had heads, and with them they do hurt' (Rev. ix. 13–19).

From the symbols employed under the fifth trumpet, viz., the locusts, we inferred that the prediction had reference to affairs in the East. We have more decisive proof of an eastern application of the prediction under the sixth trumpet; for the scene is laid expressly on the banks of the Euphrates. As the preceding trumpet set forth the ravages of the Saracen warriors, so the one before us refers, undoubtedly, to the subsequent conquests of the Turks; reaching down to the overthrow of the eastern Roman empire, and the capture of Constantinople.

The Turks, or Turkomans, were originally an horde of Tartars, having their home in the far East, and in the region of the Caspian Sea. They first invaded and conquered Persia, and a part of India, and then came in contact with the caliphs of Bagdad and Bassora. About this time they renounced their Pagan religion, and embraced the Mohammedan. For a time they were unable to cross the Euphrates and invade the countries of western Asia. The power of the caliphs prevented them. But in the year 1055, Bagdad was taken by the Turkomans, and the way was open for them to extend their victories westward. The capture of Bagdad was the event which loosed the four evil angels, which had been held back on the eastern bank of the Euphrates, and left them at liberty to pursue their conquests. They immediately crossed the river with a vast army, chiefly horsemen, the number of which John sets down as 'two hundred thousand thousand.'[1]

These are what John saw in vision,—a vast and all but numberless army. They did not rush at once to the capture of Constantinople, but passed many years in a roving, marauding course of life,—sometimes victorious and sometimes vanquished,—but getting meanwhile a foot-hold in western Asia, and gathering strength for more decisive operations. At length, after much fighting and long preparation, Constantinople was attacked. A part of it was taken by storm, and a part capitulated. In the former part, Christian worship and ordinances were at once suppressed; in the latter, they were allowed to be continued for a time. But ere long they were abolished altogether, and the venerable capital of the eastern empire became a Mohammedan city.

This event took place in the year 1453; and we are now to inquire whether the time was designated

---

Gibbon, speaking of this invasion, says: 'The myriads of Turkish horse overspread a frontier of six hundred miles.' Vol. v. p. 512.

in the prediction. After the Turkish army was let loose upon western Asia, it was to continue 'for an hour, a day, a month, and a year.' In prophetic time, this amounts to a little more than three hundred and ninety-one years. The Turks commenced their career of conquest in the year 1062. To this number add three hundred and ninety-one, and you have 1453,—the precise year in which Constantinople fell. There is some diversity of statement as to the year in which the Turks commenced their wars in eastern Asia; but the result, in every case, comes very near to that stated above. And surely it is a most remarkable result, going to assure us of the accuracy of the prediction which contains it, and of the method of interpreting this prediction.

The horses in this terrific struggle are described in the prophecy, with their 'breast-plates of fire, their heads like lions, and brimstone and smoke and fire pouring forth from their mouths.' Of course, they are not literal horses, but symbols of events taking place during the war. It is remarkable that fire-arms and cannon were first used in the assault upon Constantinople; and this is supposed to be indicated by the fire and smoke and brimstone which seemed to issue from the horses' mouths.

The design of this terrible infliction upon the heathen and nominally Christian people of western Asia, was to humble them, and bring them to con-

sideration and repentance. But no such good result flowed from it; and so it was predicted in the
verses following: 'The rest of the men which were
not killed by these plagues, yet repented not of the
works of their hands, that they should not worship
devils, and idols of gold, and silver, and brass, and
stone, and of wood; which neither can see, nor hear,
nor walk: neither repented they of their murders,
nor of their sorceries, nor of their fornication, nor of
their thefts' (Rev. ix. 20, 21)

CHAPTER VIII.

CHRIST APPEARS AS A MIGHTY ANGEL : THE END NOT YET.

REVELATION, CHAP. X.

' AND I saw another mighty angel come down from heaven, clothed with a cloud: and a rainbow was upon his head, and his face was as it were the sun, and his feet as pillars of fire ; and he had in his hand a little book open: and he set his right foot upon the sea, and his left foot on the earth, and he cried with a loud voice, as when a lion roareth . and when he had cried, seven thunders uttered their voices. And when the seven thunders had uttered their voices, I was about to write : and I heard a voice from heaven saying unto me, Seal up those things which the seven thunders uttered, and write them not. And the angel which I saw stand upon the sea and upon the earth lifted up his hand to heaven, and sware by him that liveth for ever and ever, who created heaven, and the things that therein are, and the earth, and the things that therein are, and the sea, and the things which are therein, that there should be time no

longer. (οὐχετι ἐσται, should not be yet.) But in
the days of the voice of the seventh angel, when he
shall begin to sound, the mystery of God should
be finished, as He hath declared to His servants,
the prophets. And the voice which I heard from
heaven spake unto me again, and said, Go and take
the little book which is open in the hand of the
angel which standeth upon the sea and upon the
earth. And I went unto the angel, and said unto
him, Give me the little book. And he said unto me,
Take it, and eat it up; and it shall make thy belly
bitter, but it shall be in thy mouth sweet as honey.
And I took the little book out of the angel's hand,
and ate it up; and it was in my mouth sweet as
honey: and as soon as I had eaten it, my belly
was bitter. And he said unto me, Thou must prophesy again before many peoples, and nations, and
tongues, and kings' (Rev. x.).

This glorious vision is an episode thrown into
the continuous train of prophecy. The blast of the
sixth angel was not finished with the fall of Constantinople and the Eastern empire. Probably it
is not finished now. The dominion of the Turks—
the leading subject of it—is not yet overthrown,
though apparently verging to its end. In the
midst of events portended by the sixth trumpet,
the sublime vision of this tenth chapter intervenes.

A mighty angel comes down from heaven,

'clothed with a cloud, and a rainbow about his head: his face was as it were the sun, and his feet as pillars of fire.' Who is this mighty angel? After considering the various opinions which have been offered in answer to this question, I agree with Hengstenberg, that this angel is none other than the Lord Jesus Christ. Nor is it a valid objection to this conclusion, that He is here called angel. The word angel signifies *messenger;* and in executing His mediatorial work, Christ often appears and acts as the messenger of God, and is not unfrequently called an angel.[1] He is, as it seems to me, called so here.

My first proof of the Divine character of this angel is found in the transcendant glory of his appearance,—so very like to that of his appearance to John, as recorded in the first chapter of the Revelation,—transcending in some particulars the glory even of that epiphany. Then the planting of his right foot upon the sea, and his left foot on the earth, reveals him as the rightful proprietor and sovereign of the world. And the solemn oath which he takes, shows him to be one who has the times and the seasons in his own power, to prolong, curtail, and decide, according to his pleasure.

And the little book which he held in his hand,

[1] See Gen. xvi. 7-13 ; xxi. 7-22 ; xi. 15.

what are we to think of that? This I understand
to be the remaining, unfulfilled part of the book of
prophecy, which he took out of the hand of Him
that sat upon the throne, in the early part of the
Revelation (chap. v. 7). The seals of this book had
all been opened, but the portents of the seventh seal,
which included the seven trumpets, were not yet
entirely fulfilled. The seventh trumpet had not
been blown, nor had the blast of the sixth trumpet
ceased to sound. The contents of the book which
he had received from the Supreme Disposer had
been chiefly unfolded; but a small part was yet
unaccomplished, and this constituted the little book
which he still held in his hand.

And this accounts for the effect which the eat-
ing of the book produced upon the apostle. In his
mouth it was sweet, but in his belly bitter. The
first announcement of the seventh trumpet, that
the kingdoms of this world were all given to Christ,
would be sweet indeed. But when the eater came
to understand how many ages of conflict and persecution were yet to precede the sounding of the
seventh trumpet, and what commotions and revolutions would accompany it, the sweet was turned
into bitter.

But why was this glorious vision interjected
here? Why did the Son of God condescend to
appear again as the Angel of the Covenant, and

swear the solemn oath contained in this chapter?
I can think of but one reason, and that one is
eminently honourable to the Saviour, showing His
compassion to His people, and His care for them.

As early as the close of the first century, many
excellent Christians were pleasing themselves with
the idea of the speedy coming of Christ. He was
soon to come, and set up His kingdom in the world,
and reign in glory with His saints. And this de-
lusion has been revived, at different periods, all the
way from the age of John to the present time.
During the blast of the sixth trumpet, some of the
best people on the earth were deceiving themselves
in this way. This was the case with John Wickliffe and his followers,—the Lollards, the Hussites,
and many others. Wickliffe supposed that the millennium commenced at the time of Constantine, that
the thousand years had been fulfilled, that the Fiend
(as he called him) was let loose for a little season,
and that the coming of Christ to judgment was
just at hand. Under one form or another, these adventists continued down to the time of the Reformation. They were found in many of the reformed
Churches, and even among our New England
Fathers. They are found in almost every Protestant country at the present time. Some of
them have been fanatical and heretical, but many
of them have been pious, excellent people, loving

r

the Lord Jesus, and clinging to the hope of His speedy appearing. Others who have not advanced so far as this have had their patience tried by delay. They have been ready to say, with the souls under the altar, 'How long, Holy and True, dost Thou not judge and avenge the sufferings of Thy people! How long shall it be to the end of these wonders!'

In compassion for both these descriptions of persons, and to cure them, if possible, of their impatience and delusions, their Lord presents himself in this most remarkable vision. Standing in glory upon the sea and the land, He lifts up His hand to heaven, and sweareth by Him who liveth for ever and ever, that the time of the end is not yet. But in the days of the voice of the seventh angel, when he shall begin to sound, then shall the mystery of God be finished, as He hath declared to His servants the prophets, Let him that readeth (or heareth) understand!

CHAPTER IX.

THE TESTIMONY OF THE WITNESSES—THE SEVENTH TRUMPET.

REVELATION, CHAP. XI.

' A ND there was given me a reed like unto a rod: and the angel stood, saying, Rise, and measure the temple of God, and the altar, and them that worship therein. But the court which is without the temple leave out, and measure it not; for it is given unto the Gentiles: and the holy city shall they tread under foot forty and two months. And I will give power unto my two witnesses, and they shall prophesy a thousand two hundred and threescore days, clothed in sackcloth. These are the two olive-trees, and the two candlesticks standing before the God of the earth. And if any man will hurt them, fire proceedeth out of their mouth, and devoureth their enemies; and if any man will hurt them, he must in this manner be killed. These have power to shut heaven, that it rain not in the days of their prophecy; and have power over waters to turn them into blood, and to smite the earth with plagues, as often as they will.

And when they shall have finished their testimony, the beast that ascendeth out of the bottomless pit shall make war against them, and shall overcome them, and kill them. And their dead bodies shall lie in the street of the great city, which spiritually is called Sodom and Egypt, where also our Lord was crucified. And they of the people, and kindreds, and tongues, and nations, shall see their dead bodies three days and an half, and shall not suffer their dead bodies to be put in graves. And they that dwell upon the earth shall rejoice over them, and make merry, and shall send gifts one to another; because these two prophets tormented them that dwelt on the earth. And after three days and a half the Spirit of life from God entered into them, and they stood upon their feet; and great fear fell upon them that saw them. And they heard a great voice from heaven saying unto them, Come up hither. And they ascended up to heaven in a cloud; and their enemies beheld them. And the same hour was a great earthquake, and the tenth part of the city fell, and in the earthquake were slain of men seven thousand: and the remnant were affrighted, and gave glory to the God of heaven' (Rev. xi. 1–13).

By interpreting parts of this chapter literally, some authors have inferred that Jerusalem and the Jewish temple were still standing; and, consequently, that the Apocalypse must have been written at a much earlier period than we have supposed. But there is no real ground for such a supposition. The language of the chapter before us is symbolical, —much of it certainly, and probably all. The temple and the altar spoken of in the first verse cannot be the literal temple at Jerusalem. Who can suppose that John, on the isle of Patmos, was required to take a reed, and go and measure the literal temple at Jerusalem? How could he do it? And why should he be required to do it, since the measure of the temple was accurately known? No; the temple here spoken of is a symbolic temple— the symbol of God's Church; and the command to measure it is a command to survey and estimate it, —to see how many belong to the real Church of God, and how many are to be passed by and excluded.

The command to leave out of his estimate the court without the temple, indicates that a large part of what had been considered as belonging to the Christian Church was to be regarded in this light no longer. They are left out and abandoned. Instead of belonging to Christ, they have become anti-Christ. And this I regard as a very important point in the history of the Church of Rome. For centuries it had been a Christian Church, as holy as any other in the first ages; but now it has become so corrupt as to forfeit its standing in the Church of God, and is left out of it. When was this fatal transition made? When did it occur?

I will not undertake to answer these questions now. They will come up again in the progress of this discussion. But from the period of this occurrence, whenever it may have taken place, the cause of truth and holiness was to be trodden under foot in that apostate Church, and God's faithful witnesses were to prophesy in sackcloth for the space of forty-two months, or twelve hundred and sixty days. The language here is undoubtedly prophetical, and the period indicated (which is the same in both cases) is twelve hundred and sixty years.

There will be witnesses for God and truth during all this dark period, but they will be few. They are the olive trees and candlesticks for the lighting of the world; and their light, feeble and flickering though it may be at some periods, will continue. Great power is given to these despised witnesses,— likened to that wielded by Moses and the old prophets,—not literally miraculous like theirs,—but as salutary and effective to those who love the truth, and as confounding and ruinous to those who reject it. These witnesses for God were found at their posts through all the middle ages,—the Paulicians, the Cathari, the Culdees, the Lollards, the Albigenses, the Waldenses,—holding up the light of truth, and braving the hatred and persecution of the world.

And when they shall have finished (τελεσωσι, *perfected*) their testimony in sackcloth; when they shall have continued it till the object of it is accomplished, and the time has come for a change,[1] then the beast from the bottomless pit,—of whom we now hear for the first time in the Revelation, but of whom we shall hear much in the following chapters,—shall make war upon them, and kill them, and they shall lie unburied 'in the street of that great city which is spiritually called Sodom and Egypt, where also our Lord was crucified, '[2]— referring not, perhaps, to any particular city, but to those parts of the dominion of Rome which had been most frequently reddened with martyrs' blood. And there shall be great rejoicing over them among the wicked of the earth, because they can no longer terrify or trouble them with their testimony.

But in the midst of these rejoicings, the hated witnesses are raised to life. And not only so, they are exalted to a position they never before occupied

[1] The language here does not imply that the witnesses are to continue their testimony in sackcloth to the end of the twelve hundred and sixty years, or until the sounding of the seventh trumpet. Time must be furnished toward the close of their first testimony in which they are to be slain, to be raised to life, to be exalted above the power of their enemies, and to pursue their work in a more peaceful way.

[2] Dean Alford and Hengstenberg both show conclusively that the literal Jerusalem is not intended here.

—where their enemies can afflict and destroy them no more.

These witnesses, I have said already, are the faithful who, through all the years of Papal darkness, did not cease to protest against existing evils, and lift up their voice like a trumpet to reprove them. And as the time of their testimony in sackcloth drew to a close, they were assailed with unwonted violence. Their enemies were determined to silence them, or destroy them. Wars were urged against them; crusades were got up for their destruction; the Inquisition was ever at its work, and in the short period of four years is said to have destroyed one hundred and fifty thousand persons.

At length, as we approach the time of the Protestant Reformation, Rome ventured to proclaim that her work of destruction was accomplished. At the ninth session of the Council of the Lateran, held in Rome in the year 1513, a remarkable proclamation was made, affirming that all opposition to the Papal power had now ceased. The orator of the session ascended the pulpit, and affirmed: 'There is an end of resistance to the Papal rule and religion! Opposers there exist no more! The whole body of Christianity is now seen to be subject to its rightful Head'—the Pope.

It is probably from this time that the three days

and a half, or the three years and a half, during which the dead bodies of the witnesses remained unburied, and were exposed to public gaze and derision, are to be reckoned. And it is wonderful to record, that in three years and a half from the date of the above proclamation—that is, in 1517, Luther commenced his attack upon Roman Indulgences, life entered again the bodies of the dead witnesses, and the Protestant Reformation commenced.

This was followed by 'a great earthquake,'—a great moral and spiritual revolution—which shook the Papal power to its centre, and emancipated half Europe. This, too, raised the dead witnesses above the rage and the power of their enemies. They testified no longer, as before, in sackcloth and in fear of their lives, but lifted up their voices in the high places of the earth, and in the palaces of kings. 'And many were terrified, and gave glory to the God of heaven.' Yes, many were converted from the error of their ways, and from being the enemies of Christ and His people, became His friends.

'The second woe is past; and, behold, the third woe cometh quickly' (Rev. xi. 14).

The Seventh Trumpet.

'And the seventh angel sounded; and there were great voices in heaven, saying, The kingdoms of this world are become the kingdoms of our Lord, and of His Christ; and He shall reign for

Q

ever and ever. And the four and twenty elders, which sat before God on their seats, fell upon their faces, and worshipped God, saying, We give Thee thanks, O Lord God Almighty, which art, and wast, and art to come; because Thou hast taken to Thee Thy great power, and hast reigned. And the nations were angry, and Thy wrath is come, and the time of the dead, that they should be judged, and that Thou shouldest give reward unto Thy servants the prophets, and to the saints, and them that fear Thy name, small and great; and shouldest destroy them which destroy the earth. And the temple of God was opened in heaven, and there was seen in His temple the ark of His testament : and there were lightnings, and voices, and thunderings, and an earthquake, and great hail' (Rev. xi. 15–19).

We have here the winding up of the first series of visions in the Revelation—those contained in the book which the Lamb took out of the hand of Him who sat upon the throne, as recorded in the fifth chapter. The Seven Seals have all been opened, and the last of the Seven Trumpets contained under the seventh seal has been blown.

This introduces us to scenes which are yet in the future. It closes the testimony of the witnesses, in the sense of the preceding vision. They had been slain, and raised from the dead, and exalted to a state of comparative security at

the time of the Reformation; but now their war-
fare is ended; their triumph is complete. The
twelve hundred and sixty years, so often spoken
of in the Revelation, is closed, and the millennial
period of the Church is ushered in; when 'the kingdom, and dominion, and greatness of the kingdoms
under the whole heaven shall be given to the people
of the saints of the Most High.'

This seventh trumpet, though a joyful one to the
people of God, is called a *woe-trumpet*, on account of
its bearing upon His enemies; portending the destruction of their power, the defeat of all their plans,
and their subjection, for a long period, to the rule
of Christ and His people. 'The time of the dead'
—the spiritually dead—'is come, that they should
be judged, and that . . . . Thou shouldest destroy
them which destroy the earth.'

This is followed by one of those out-bursting
exclamations of gratitude and praise, which are so
often sounded forth in heaven, in celebrating the
victories of God and the Lamb. 'We give Thee
thanks, O Lord God Almighty, which art, and wast,
and art to come: because Thou hast taken to Thee
Thy great power, and hast reigned,' and hast given
'reward unto Thy servants the prophets, and to the
saints, and to them that fear Thy name, small and
great.'

In response to this loyal, grateful song, the

temple of God was opened in heaven—opened even to the holy of holies, so that the ark of the testament was seen: 'And there were lightnings, and thunderings, and an earthquake and great hail.' These symbols portend the great changes and revolutions that must take place on the earth, when all the wicked are converted or destroyed, and the kingdom and dominion are given to the saints.

CHAPTER X.

THE MYSTICAL WOMAN AND HER SEED.
REVELATION, CHAP. XII.

'AND there appeared a great wonder in heaven; a woman clothed with the sun, and the moon under her feet, and upon her head a crown of twelve stars: And she, being with child, cried, travailing in birth, and pained to be delivered. And there appeared another wonder in heaven; and behold a great red dragon, having seven heads and ten horns, and seven crowns upon his heads. And his tail drew the third part of the stars of heaven, and did cast them to the earth: and the dragon stood before the woman which was ready to be delivered, for to devour her child as soon as it was born. And she brought forth a man-child, who was to rule all nations with a rod of iron: And her child was caught up unto God, and to His throne. And the woman fled into the wilderness, where she hath a place prepared of God, that they should feed her there a thousand two hundred and threescore days.

'And there was war in heaven: Michael and his angels fought against the dragon; and the dragon fought and his angels, and prevailed not; neither was their place found any more in heaven. And the great dragon was cast out, that old serpent, called the Devil, and Satan, which deceiveth the whole world: he was cast out into the earth, and his angels were cast out with him. And I heard a loud voice saying in heaven, Now is come salvation, and strength, and the kingdom of our God, and the power of His Christ: for the accuser of our brethren is cast down, which accused them before our God day and night. And they overcame him by the blood of the Lamb, and by the word of their testimony; and they loved not their lives unto the death. Therefore rejoice, ye heavens, and ye that dwell in them.

'Woe to the inhabiters of the earth and of the sea! for the devil is come down unto you, having great wrath, because he knoweth that he hath but a short time.

'And when the dragon saw that he was cast unto the earth, he persecuted the woman which brought forth the man-child. And to the woman were given two wings of a great eagle, that she might fly into the wilderness, into her place, where she is nourished for a time, and times, and half a time'—three years and an half, or twelve hundred and sixty days—

'from the face of the serpent. And the serpent cast out of his mouth water as a flood, after the woman, that he might cause her to be carried away of the flood. And the earth helped the woman; and the earth opened her mouth, and swallowed up the flood which the dragon cast out of his mouth. And the dragon was wroth with the woman, and went to make war with the remnant of her seed, which keep the commandments of God, and have the testimony of Jesus Christ' (Rev. xii.).

Having closed the first series of visions in the Apocalypse—those connected with the book of seven seals—we now enter upon a consideration of other visions,—some of them running back and covering a part of the ground over which we have already passed.

In this twelfth chapter, John has a vision, the scene of which is laid in the visible heavens—the region of the sun, moon, and stars—and not, as before, in the celestial heavens. He sees a royally attired woman, bathed as it were in the light of the sun, with the moon under her feet, and twelve stars, like a coronal, encircling her head. She is in travail, and brings forth a son.

This woman and her seed, undoubtedly, represents the Church of Christ, looking back to its origin in the first ages. Her progeny is in peril before its birth; for there is crouched very near her 'a great

red dragon, having seven heads and ten horns.' He
is a fearful monster, lying along the sky, and seeming to beat down, with the thrash of his tail, a third
part of the stars of heaven.   He is watching the
travailing woman, and waiting to destroy her child
as soon as it is born.

This shows the perils of the Church of Christ
in its early history, and the watchful intent of the
powers of darkness to destroy it; for this great red
dragon is expressly interpreted to be 'that old serpent, called the Devil, and Satan.'   But he is foiled
in his attempt to seize and destroy the child.   The
babe is instantly taken to a place of security, and
the mother flies into the wilderness, where a place
is prepared for her, and where she is to be protected
and nourished for twelve hundred and sixty days,
or years,—the same period in which the witnesses
are said to have borne their testimony.

Defeated in his designs upon the early Church,
Satan and his legions now engage in open conflict
with the archangel Michael and his legions.   John
saw this conflict in the visible heavens,—much like
one which is said to have been witnessed over Jerusalem, just previous to its overthrow by Titus.[1]   Of
course, the whole scene was emblematic and vision-
ary, showing the deep interest which invisible beings,
good and bad, feel in the destinies of men; some

---

[1] See Tacitus, Book v. sect. 13.

striving for their salvation, and others as intently, for their destruction.

In this conflict the dragon is defeated, driven out of the visible heavens, and cast down to the earth. Still, his hatred of the mystical woman, the Church, is not abated. He pursues her into the place of her retirement, and because he cannot overtake her, he pours forth after her a flood of water to destroy her. But her Almighty protector is prepared for this attempt. He opens chasms in the affrighted earth, which swallow up the rushing waters, and the Church is safe. She is protected and nourished for the long period above stated,—the twelve hundred and sixty years.

And now, what more instructive parable could have been invented to set forth the hatred of wicked beings, satanic and human, to the Church of Christ, with their persistent efforts to destroy it, and at the same time to signify its safety in the hands of its great Deliverer? He thwarts every effort, defeats every design for its destruction, until, in the fulness of time, in the end of these wonders, it is brought out into a large place, and its final victory is secured.

It is said in the prediction, that the Church will one day rule the guilty nations 'with a rod of iron,' or an iron sceptre. This phraseology, as we find it in the Scriptures, does not imply cruelty or injustice,

but merely firmness, invincibleness, and integrity.
It is applied, in more than one instance, to the rule
of the Messiah (Rev. xix. 15; Ps. ii. 9).

We have, mixed up with the triumphs of this
vision, as of the last, loud voices in heaven, saying,
'Now is come salvation, and strength, and the
kingdom of our God, and the power of His Christ:
for the accuser of our brethren is cast down. . . .
And they overcame him by the blood of the Lamb,
and by the word of their testimony; and they loved
not their lives unto the death' (Rev. xii. 10, 11).

CHAPTER XI.

RISE AND DESCRIPTION OF THE PAPAL BEASTS.

REVELATION, CHAP. XIII.

' AND I stood upon the sand of the sea, and saw a beast rise up out of the sea, having seven heads and ten horns, and upon his horns ten crowns, and upon his heads the name of blasphemy. And the beast which I saw was like unto a leopard, and his feet were as the feet of a bear, and his mouth as the mouth of a lion: and the dragon gave him his power, and his seat, and great authority. And I saw one of his heads as it were wounded to death; and his deadly wound was healed: and all the world wondered after the beast. And they worshipped the dragon which gave power unto the beast: and they worshipped the beast, saying, Who is like unto the beast? who is able to make war with him? And there was given unto him a mouth speaking great things, and blasphemies · and power was given unto him to continue forty and two months. And he opened his mouth in blasphemy against God, to blaspheme His name, and His tabernacle, and them that dwell in heaven. And it was given unto him to make war with the saints, and to overcome them: and power was given him over all kindreds, and tongues, and nations. And all that dwell upon the earth shall worship him, whose names are not written in the book of life of the Lamb slain from the foundation of the world. If any man have an ear, let him hear. He that leadeth into captivity, shall go into captivity: he that killeth with the sword, must be killed with the sword. Here is the patience and the faith of the saints' (Rev. xiii. 1–10).

The beast of the Apocalypse was incidentally mentioned in chap. vii. 11; but here he is fully presented and described. A beast, in prophetic language, represents a tyrannical, idolatrous kingdom, or power. Such were the several beasts which Daniel saw rising up from the sea. The kingdom of God and of Christ is never set before us under the symbol of a beast.

As John stood on the sea shore of Patmos, he ' saw a beast rise up out of the sea, having seven heads and ten horns, and upon his horns ten crowns, and upon his heads the names of blasphemy,' or blasphemous names.

The seven heads and ten horns mark this beast as Rome, in its *civil secular power*. The seven heads denote the seven hills on which Rome was built, and the seven forms of government which successively prevailed there. The first six of these, according to Tacitus, were Kings, Consuls, Dictators, Decemvirs, Military Tribunes, and Emperors; five of which had passed away before the time of this prophecy; and the sixth form, the Imperial, was then in its glory. But this, before the fulfilment of the prophecy, had been wounded to death, and the deadly wound had been healed.

Its wounding and healing are thus set forth in history. Rome ceased to be an empire in the year 476, when Augustulus, the last of the emperors, was conquered by Odoacer, king of the Goths. From this period Rome continued to be subject to foreign princes for about three hundred years. During a part of this time it was reduced to a mere dukedom, and made subject to the Exarch of Ravenna. This, surely, was a wounding to death of the sixth or imperial head of Rome.

In the latter part of the sixth century the Lombards broke into Italy, possessed themselves of a considerable part of it, and established a kingdom at Pavia. As they increased in ambition and strength, they strove to become masters of Ravenna and Rome. In these circumstances, the Popes of Rome applied, first to Pepin, king of the Franks, and afterwards to his son, Charlemagne, for help. The Franks came into Italy at two separate times, drove out the Lombards, and gave their dominions to the Pope.   They thus constituted the bishop of Rome a monarch.   He was the sovereign of Rome, and of a considerable part of Italy; and here was the origin of the temporal dominions of the Pope (of which he has recently been divested).   Here was the healing of the wounded imperial head; the head was restored in another form, and it continued to be a reigning power for the next thousand years.

But the beast which John saw had not only seven heads, but ten crowned horns.   These signify the ten kingdoms into which, on its being broken up, the western Roman empire was divided.

It follows that the beast which John saw rising out of the sea was not Pagan Rome, nor imperial Rome, but Papal Rome.   It was Rome after its imperial head had been wounded to death by the incursions of the Goths—after it had been divided into ten separate governments or kingdoms—and after its deadly wound had been healed by crowning the Pontiff, and making him sovereign of a considerable part of Italy.   It was this imperial *Papal* Rome which afterwards ' opened its mouth in blasphemy against God, to blaspheme His name, and His tabernacle, and them that dwell in heaven.' It was this power which ' made war with the saints, and overcame them,' and which all the wicked of the earth have been inclined to follow and to worship.   And this same power was to continue its blasphemous course and bloody career for forty and two months, or twelve hundred and sixty days, or to the end of the twelve hundred and sixty years. And then its retribution should come; he that had led so many into captivity, should go into captivity; and he that had killed so many by the sword, should be killed by the sword.

'And I beheld another beast coming up out of the earth, and he had two horns like a lamb, and he spake as a dragon: and he exerciseth all the power of the first beast before him, and causeth the earth, and them that dwell therein, to worship the first beast, whose deadly wound was healed. And he doeth great wonders, so that he maketh fire come down from heaven on the earth in the sight of men, and deceiveth them that dwell on the earth by the means of those miracles which he had power to do in the sight of the beast, saying to them that dwell on the earth, that they should make an image to the beast, which had the wound by a sword, and did live. And he had power to give life unto the image of the beast, that the image of the beast should both speak, and cause that as many as would not worship the image of the beast should be killed. And he caused all, both small and great, rich and poor, free and bond, to receive a mark in their right hand, or in their foreheads: and that no man might buy or sell, save

he that had the mark, or the name of the beast, or
the number of his name.   Here is wisdom, Let
him that hath understanding count the number of
the beast: for it is the number of a man; and
his number is six hundred three score and six'
(Rev. xiii. 11–18).

If we have succeeded in giving the true significance of the first beast, there can be no mistake
in regard to the second: for the two are evidently
in close alliance, mutual assistants, working together for the same objects and designs.   The
second beast ' exerciseth all the power of the first
beast before him, and causeth the earth, and them
that dwell therein, to worship the first beast, whose
deadly wound was healed.'   At the same time, he
has not the same fierce look as the first beast.
He has horns like a lamb, though he speaks as a
dragon.   In short, if the first beast was Papal
Rome, in its *secular kingly* authority, the second is
the same Papal Rome in its alleged *spiritual ecclesiastical* authority.   The two things are distinct, as
here represented, and yet they cannot be separated.
They run on together, playing into each other's
hands, and yielding a mutual countenance and support, until they come to the end of their career;
which is, the end of the twelve hundred and sixty
years.

The second beast claims, as the Church of Rome

has ever done, the power to work miracles. 'He doeth great wonders, so that he maketh fire come down from heaven on the earth in the sight of men, and deceiveth them that dwell on the earth by means of those miracles which he had power to do in the sight of the beast.' These are false miracles, of course, or men would not be *deceived* by them.

The second beast, like the first, is a persecutor. He 'causeth that as many as will not worship the image of the first beast, shall be killed.' He sets his mark on all his followers, and will not allow them to traffic with those who have not the mark, or the name of the beast, or the number of his name.

As this device of Popery is not so generally understood as some others, I adduce the following authorities to prove it. The Council of Lateran, under Pope Alexander III., has a severe canon against the Albigenses and Waldenses. It anathematises any one 'who should receive or cherish them in his house, or have traffic with them.' The synod of Tours, under the same Pope, commands that no one 'should receive or assist these heretics, or hold any communion with them in selling or buying, that so, being deprived of the comforts of life, they may be compelled to repent of the errors of their way.' Also Pope Martin v., in his bull, issued after the Council of Con-

S

stance, enjoins upon his people that they shall not allow ' the heretics to have houses in their districts, or to enter into any contracts, or carry on commerce, or enjoy the comforts of humanity with Christians.'

In short, there is no difficulty in seeing what power is represented by this second beast, even if the closing test proposed by the writer be not applied. This closing test is the number of his name ; and this, says John, ' is six hundred three score and six.'

Various interpretations have been put upon this number, but nearly all of them terminate in Rome. The one given by Irenæus, who lived near the time of John, is as likely to be correct as any other. He represents the Greek letters, which, used as numerals, amount to 666, as also forming the word ΛΑΤΕΙΝΟΣ, (*Latinus*), which is but another name for Rome.

Others solve the mystery of the number in another way. They show that the time between the vision in the chapter before us, and the commencement of the Pope's kingly authority, was 666 years.

In our previous inquiry we have found frequent mention of the forty and two months and twelve hundred and sixty days,—which we understand to denote twelve hundred and sixty years,—in which the Church is to be persecuted and well-nigh destroyed by its enemies. Thus, the holy city is to be trodden under foot forty and two months; and the two witnesses are to prophesy in sackcloth twelve hundred and sixty days (chap. xi. 2, 3). The mystical woman is to flee into the wilderness, and be nourished there twelve hundred and sixty days (chap. xii. 6, 14). And the beast rising out of the sea is to continue his iron rule forty and two months (chap. xiii. 5). So, in Daniel, the saints of the Most High are to be given into the hands of the power represented by the little horn, until 'a time and times, and the dividing of time,' *i.e.*, three years and a half—the same period as that indicated in the Revelation (Dan. vii. 25).

The question arises now, When did this long period of oppression and persecution commence? And when will it end?

It ends, in every case, in what is technically called the millennium. And if we knew with accuracy when it commenced, we might determine the date of the millennium. But this we do not know. When was the mystical temple measured, and the court of the Gentiles left out, and the holy city given up to be trodden under foot? When did the two witnesses commence giving their testimony in sackcloth? When did the woman flee into the wilderness, to be sheltered and nourished there? When were the saints of the Most

High given into the hands of Daniel's little horn? We have not the means of answering definitely any of these questions. Perhaps the periods indicated by them did not all commence together, but at different times, in the course of a century or more. Papal Rome did not rise to the height of its supremacy all at once. Its usurpations were gradually assumed. Its abominations were gradually accumulated; and so its prostration and breaking up may be gradual. The millennium may not be fully introduced at once. It may come along gradually, and in some of its stages imperceptibly Its light, which even now may be streaking the east, will shine brighter and brighter unto the perfect day.

There is, however, one of the Apocalyptic symbols denoting the commencement of the twelve hundred and sixty years, which, as it seems to me, is quite definitely fixed,—I mean the rising of the beast out of the sea, in the thirteenth chapter. This beast, we have seen, denotes Papal Rome, in its political secular character; and it arose when the Pope received his temporal dominions, and became a king. This took place about the year 756; and the twelve hundred and sixty years added to this, will make the millennium to commence in about A.D. 2000, or in the six thousandth year of the world. Meanwhile, the way will be constantly preparing for it; revolutions will be taking place, one after another; and the power of Rome will be constantly diminishing. But at the time above mentioned, the millennium, I trust, may be fully introduced, and the seven thousandth year of the world may be its great Sabbatical period.

I have said that this period—the twelve hundred and sixty years—in every mention of it, terminates with the millennium. So also does that long series of prophecies contained in the sealed book. The seven trumpets are all of them included under the seventh seal; and when the seventh trumpet was sounded, great voices were heard in heaven, saying, ' The kingdoms of this world are become the kingdoms of our Lord and of His Christ, and He shall reign for ever and ever.' The millennial period had now fully come.

I may further add, that all the predictions in the Revelation preceding the twentieth chapter, terminate in the millennium. None of them look beyond it. This consideration may help to a satisfactory solution of the symbols in some of the following chapters.

CHAPTER XII.

DANIEL'S VISION OF THE FOUR BEASTS.

DANIEL, CHAP. VII.

THE resemblance between some parts of Daniel's vision of the four beasts, recorded in Daniel, chapter vii., and John's vision of the Papal beasts, of which we have spoken, is so striking and illustrative, that we shall be indulged in calling attention to it in this supplementary chapter.

The vision of the four beasts is, perhaps, the most remarkable of Daniel's visions. He was favoured with it in the first year of Belshazzar, king of Babylon. 'I saw in my vision by night,' says Daniel, 'and, behold, the four winds of the heaven strove upon the great sea. And four great beasts came up from the sea, diverse one from another. The first was like a lion, and had eagle's wings: I beheld till the wings thereof were plucked, and it was lifted up from the earth, and made stand upon the feet as a man, and a man's heart was given to it. And behold another beast, a second, like to a bear, and it raised up itself on one side, and it had three ribs in the mouth of it between the teeth of it;

and they said thus unto it, Arise, devour much flesh. After this I beheld, and lo another, like a leopard, which had upon the back of it four wings of a fowl; the beast had also four heads; and dominion was given to it. After this I saw in the night visions, and behold a fourth beast, dreadful and terrible, and strong exceedingly; and it had great iron teeth: it devoured and brake in pieces, and stamped the residue with the feet of it: and it was diverse from all the beasts that were before it; and it had ten horns. I considered the horns, and, behold, there came up among them another little horn, before whom there were three of the first horns plucked up by the roots: and, behold, in this horn were eyes like the eyes of a man, and a mouth speaking great things' (Dan. vii. 2–8).

Daniel beheld this terrible beast until it was brought to judgment, was slain, and his body given to the burning flame. Following this was the universal prevalence of Christ's kingdom, or what we call the millennium: 'And there was given Him dominion, and glory, and a kingdom, that all people, nations, and languages, should serve Him: His dominion is an everlasting dominion, which shall not pass away, and His kingdom that which shall not be destroyed' (Dan. vii. 14).

A celestial visitant now comes forward, and interprets the vision to Daniel. The first three beasts represent the first three great kingdoms of the ancient world, the Babylonian, the Medo-Persian, and the Grecian. The fourth beast represents, I can have no doubt, the vast empire of Rome. 'This,' says the angel, 'shall be diverse from all kingdoms, and shall devour the whole earth, and shall tread it down, and break it in pieces. And the ten horns out of this kingdom are ten kings that shall arise: and another shall arise after them; and he shall be diverse from the first, and he shall subdue three kings. And he shall speak great words against the Most High, and shall wear out the saints of the Most High, and think to change times and laws: and they'—the saints—'shall be given into his hand until a time and times and the dividing of time. But the judgment shall sit, and they shall take away his dominion, to consume and destroy it unto the end. And the kingdom and dominion, and the greatness of the kingdom under the whole heaven, shall be given to the people of the saints of the Most High, whose kingdom is an everlasting kingdom, and all dominions shall serve and obey Him' (Dan. vii. 23–27).

I am aware that some interpreters make Daniel's fourth beast to denote the four kingdoms growing out of the empire of Alexander the Great, and the little horn to represent that great oppressor of the Jews, Antiochus Epiphanes. But to this supposition there are insuperable objections. It obliges us, in the first

place, to separate these four kingdoms from the empire of Alexander; whereas Daniel represents them
as part and parcel of it, and organically connected
with it. 'Therefore the he goat (Alexander) waxed
very great: and when he was strong, the great
horn was broken; and from it came up four notable
horns,' springing, of course, out of the head of *the
same beast* (Dan. viii. 8). How then can they be
made to constitute another beast?

Then Daniel's fourth beast has ten horns, which,
on the Antiochian theory, we fail to find. The
advocates of this theory suppose them to be the
kings of Syria and Egypt, who reigned previous to
Antiochus; but of these there were thirteen, and
not ten. Besides, the little horn of the fourth
beast is represented as springing up while the
other horns were standing; whereas the pre-
decessors of Antiochus on the thrones of Syria and
Egypt were all dead before it appeared. Then
Daniel represents three of the existing horns as
plucked up by the little horn—a condition which
it is impossible to apply to Antiochus.

The reasons for supposing Daniel's fourth beast
to represent the empire of Rome are the following :—[1]

---

[1] Luther says, 'All the world is unanimous in this interpretation,'
viz., that the fourth beast of Daniel represents the empire of Rome.
See Auberlen on Daniel and Revelations, p. 168.

1. The beast, in its terrible aspect, and especially in the number of its horns, is very like to the beast which John saw rising out of the sea, and which we have seen, represents Papal Rome (Rev. xiii. 1).

2. Then *the great strength* of Daniel's fourth beast is much insisted on. It is 'dreadful, and terrible, and strong exceedingly.' It 'devours, and breaks in pieces, and stamps the residue with its feet.' It 'shall devour the whole earth,' says the interpreting angel, 'and tread it down, and break it in pieces' (Dan. vii. 7, 23). In a parallel passage, Daniel says: 'The fourth kingdom shall be strong as iron: forasmuch iron breaketh in pieces and subdueth all things' (Dan. ii. 40). Now, all this applies exactly to the great Roman empire, but not at all to the kingdoms of Alexander's successors, or to any of them.

3. Regarding these kingdoms as organically connected with the Grecian empire, as Daniel certainly did, then the Roman empire follows immediately upon the fall of the great Grecian empire; as that of Alexander did upon the fall of the Medo-Persian empire, and the Medo-Persian upon the fall of the Babylonian. Indeed, it was Rome which engulfed and swallowed up the poor remains of the Grecian empire. In this view, the four great empires follow each other consecutively and analogically.

4. The Roman empire had much to do with *the*

Church of God, both before and after the coming of Christ. Hence there is the same reason why Rome should be noted in this notable prophecy, as why Babylon, or Persia, or Alexander and his successors, should be.

5. But the grand reason why we regard the fourth beast of Daniel as setting forth the Roman empire is, that its ultimate downfall, in Papal Rome, is immediately followed, as I have said before, by the millennial kingdom. No sooner is 'its dominion taken away, to consume and destroy it unto the end,' than 'the kingdom, and dominion, and greatness of the kingdom under the whole heaven is given to the people of the saints of the Most High' (Dan. vii. 27). This, it seems to me, is decisive as to the interpretation of the fourth beast. Antiochus Epiphanes died one hundred and sixty four years before the coming of Christ. But Daniel's fourth beast is to retain and exert his terrific power long ages after the Christian era; and, upon his final destruction, the millennial glory of the Church is to be ushered in.

It should be kept in mind that two little horns are brought before us in the predictions of Daniel. One springs from the roots of 'the king of Grecia,' and denotes, undoubtedly, the cruel and blasphemous Antiochus Epiphanes (see Dan. viii. 9–12.) The other springs from the head of Daniel's fourth beast.

It comes up in connection with Rome, and in the doctrine of the vast Roman dominion. It clearly represents the Papacy in its *temporal power*. The springing up of this horn, and the rising of John's first beast out of the sea, in Rev. xiii. 1, refer to the same event—the rise of the Papal kingdom.

Daniel presents us with one fact in regard to this Papal kingdom which John does not mention, viz., that three of the existing ten kingdoms were overthrown in order to make room for it. Sir Isaac Newton says, and in his judgment we coincide, that these three were the government of Rome itself, the kingdom of the Lombards, and the Exarchate of Ravenna. These three governments were subverted by Pepin and Charlemagne, and their territory given to the Pontiff, to constitute his temporal kingdom.

This little horn, or Papal Rome, is said to have 'eyes like a man, and a mouth speaking great things,' 'He shall speak great words against the Most High, and shall wear out the saints of the Most High,' making war with them, and prevailing against them. 'He shall think to change times and laws,'— to abolish existing ordinances and establish new ones, according to his pleasure. He is to continue 'a time, times, and the dividing of time'—three years and a half [1]—in prophetic lan-

---

[1] A time in Daniel signifies a year (Dan. iv. 16).

guage, twelve hundred and sixty years,—the same period as the beast of John. And then the judgment shall sit, and 'they shall take away his dominion, to consume and destroy it unto the end.' Upon this follows immediately, as in the Revelation, the millennial kingdom. 'The kingdom, and dominion, and the greatness of the kingdom under the whole heaven, is given to the people of the saints of the Most High.'

Such coincidences in the predictions of these two great prophets,—living under different dispensations and so remote from each other,—are certainly very remarkable and instructive. They serve to confirm our faith in the inspiration of both, and our confidence in the correctness of those interpretations which have been put upon them.

CHAPTER XIII.

SUNDRY VISIONS—PREPARATION FOR THE SEVEN LAST PLAGUES.

REVELATION, CHAPS. XIV., XV.

THE visions in this chapter are of a miscellaneous character, some of which have no prophetical significance. From the prolonged ravages of the beasts in the preceding chapter, the eye of the seer is now directed to heaven.

'I looked, and, lo, a Lamb stood on the mount Sion, and with him a hundred and forty-four thousand,'—a definite number for an indefinite, —' having his Father's name written on their foreheads. And I heard a voice from heaven, as the voice of many waters, and as the voice of a great thunder: and I heard the voice of harpers harping with their harps: And they sung as it were a new song before the throne, and before the four living creatures, and the elders, and no man could learn that song but the hundred and forty and four thousand, which were redeemed from the earth. These are they which follow the Lamb whithersoever he goeth. And in their mouth was found no guile: for they are without fault before the throne of God' (Rev. xiv. 1–5).

Next, the prophet sees 'another angel fly in the midst of heaven, having the everlasting gospel to preach unto them that dwell on the earth, and to every nation, and kindred, and tongue, and people, saying, with a loud voice, Fear God and give glory to Him; for the hour of His judgment is come: and worship Him that made heaven and earth and the sea, and the fountains of waters' (Rev. xiv. 6, 7).

Among the indispensable preparations for millennial glory is the universal spread of the gospel. The gospel must first be preached among all nations. This great preparatory work is portended in the vision before us. This prediction began to be fulfilled at the time of the Reformation, when the gospel was extensively proclaimed and embraced. It is in process of fulfilment at the present day, and will be more illustriously accomplished as the millennium approaches.

Another angel immediately follows, announcing, by anticipation, that the dread conflict is over. 'Babylon is fallen, is fallen, that great city, because she made all nations drink of the wine of the wrath of her fornication' (Rev. xiv. 8).

It is no uncommon thing for the prophets to speak of events as passing, or already past, which are sure, in their time, to be accomplished. Thus, in predicting the destruction of the literal Babylon, which in his day was far future, Isaiah says: 'Bel boweth down; Nebo stoopeth; their idols are upon the beasts and the cattle: they are gone into captivity' (Isa. xlvi. 1).

Next follows an angel with a message of solemn, awful warning. 'If any man worship the beast and his image, and receive his mark in his forehead and in his head, the same shall drink of the wine of the wrath of God, which is poured out without mixture into the cup of his indignation; and he shall be tormented with fire and brimstone in the presence of the holy angels, and in the presence of the Lamb; and the smoke of their torment ascendeth up for ever and ever; and they have no rest day nor night, who worship the beast and his image, and whosoever receiveth the mark of his name' (Rev. xiv. 9–11).

This warning implies,—what is true, and what we see taking place in every direction around us,— that, in the great conflict preceding the millennium, the most strenuous efforts will be made by the emissaries of Rome to draw individuals and peoples into its interest—to impress upon them the mark of the beast, and of his image, and his name. The angel sets before them the dreadful consequences of yielding to such persuasions, and urges them to resist by every motive of terror and of fear.[1] At the same time, the warning angel proceeds to set forth the safety of those who put their trust in Christ, and patiently wait for Him. 'Here is the patience of the saints. Here are they that keep the commandments of God and the faith of Jesus' (Rev. xiv. 12).

The next vision in the chapter is one of surpassing interest. 'I looked, and behold, a white cloud, and upon the cloud one sat like unto the Son of man,'—the Lord Jesus Christ—'having on his head a golden crown, and in His hand a sharp sickle.' And a message comes to Him from the recesses of the temple: 'Thrust in Thy sickle, and reap: for the time is come for Thee to reap; for the harvest of the earth is ripe. And He that sat on the cloud thrust in his sickle on the earth, and the earth was reaped' (Rev. xiv. 14–16).

Here we behold the Son of man reaping and garnering His own chosen people, and thus securing them from the destruction which is speedily to be poured upon the wicked of the earth. And in this view, these verses seem to connect with that which precedes them: 'Blessed are the dead which die in the Lord from henceforth.' Those who die in the Lord in those troublous times are peculiarly blessed; for, being gathered and garnered by the

---

[1] The angels of heaven are not afraid of preaching terror.

U

Lord himself, no evil can overtake them. ' They shall rest from their labours (χοπων, griefs, sorrows) and their works do follow them.'

And now follows the closing vision of the chapter—one of terrible import to the wicked of the earth. It runs down obviously to the closing conflict before the millennium, and corresponds to the five last verses of the nineteenth chapter of the Revelation. ' And another angel came out of the temple which is in heaven, he also having a sharp sickle. And another angel came out from the altar, which had power over fire; and cried with a loud cry to him that had the sharp sickle, saying, Thrust in thy sharp sickle, and gather the clusters of the vine of the earth; for her grapes are fully ripe. And the angel thrust in his sickle into the earth, and gathered the vine of the earth, and cast it into the great winepress of the wrath of God. And the winepress was trodden without the city, and blood came out of the winepress, even unto the horse bridles, by the space of a thousand and six hundred furlongs' (or two hundred miles) (Rev. xiv. 17–20).

Here is presented a lake of blood, up to the horses' bridles, and two hundred miles square. Without supposing anything like a literal fulfilment, the symbols unmistakably indicate a terrible destruction of the enemies of God, to be accomplished when the harvest of the world is ripe, immediately preceding Christ's millennial kingdom.

The Seven Last Plagues.

' And I saw another sign,' or symbol, ' in heaven, great and marvellous, seven angels having the seven last plagues; for in them is filled up the wrath of God' (Rev. xv. 1).

Every reader of the Revelation must have noticed that the number seven here is of frequent occurrence. It was regarded by the Hebrews as symbolic, denoting *completeness* or *perfection*. Thus, ' the seven Spirits of God before the throne' (chap. iv. 5), denote God's perfect Holy Spirit. The seven seals include a complete system of prophecy, extending from the time of the writer to the millennium. The seven trumpets set forth a perfect series of judgments, by which the entire Roman empire, Western and Eastern, was overthrown. And the seven last plagues, in the verse before us, signify another series of judgments, by which Papal Rome will be utterly crushed, and the kingdom of Christ will be established, and become universal. They are spoken of as ' the seven last plagues ;' for in them *is filled up the wrath of God.* This indicates that they reach down to the close of the final conflict, and that there is nought, in the way of judgment, to come after them.

' And I saw as it were a sea of glass mingled

with fire; and them that had gotten the victory over the beast, and over his image, and over his mark, and over the number of his name, stand on the sea of glass, having the harps of God. And they sing the song of Moses, the servant of God, and the song of the Lamb, saying, Great and marvellous are Thy works, Lord God Almighty; just and true are Thy ways, Thou King of saints. Who shall not fear Thee, O Lord, and glorify Thy name? for Thou only art holy: for all nations shall come and worship before Thee; for Thy judgments are made manifest' (Rev. xv. 2–4).

This sea of glass, as I have before said (chap. iv. 6), does not indicate a collection of water, but rather a glossy, glittering pavement, smooth as the surface of a lake, extended round about the throne, on which those stood, with their harps, who had gotten the victory over the beast. And here they unite, as above, in singing the song of Moses and the Lamb.

'And after that I looked, and, behold, the temple of the tabernacle of the testimony in heaven was opened.' The heavenly temple was opened even to the holy of holies, where was the ark of the testimony and the mercy seat. 'And the seven angels came out of the temple,'—the inmost recesses of the temple, from the immediate presence of God, —'having the seven plagues, clothed in pure and white linen, and having their breasts girded with golden girdles.   And one of the four living creatures gave unto the seven angels seven golden vials, full of the wrath of God, who liveth for ever and ever.' The word here rendered vials signifies *bowls* or goblets.   They were filled with the implements or instruments of divine wrath.   ' And the temple was filled with smoke from the glory of God; and no man was able to enter into the temple,'—to make intercession for the guilty,—' till the seven plagues of the seven angels were fulfilled' (Rev. xv. 5–8).

CHAPTER XIV.

THE POURING OUT OF THE SEVEN VIALS.
REVELATION, CHAP. XVI.

' AND I heard a great voice out of the temple, saying to the seven angels, Go your ways and pour out the vials of the wrath of God upon the earth ' (Rev. xvi. 1).

It has been often remarked that there is a striking correspondence between the phraseology used in reference to the pouring out of these vials, and that connected with the sounding of the trumpets in the eighth and ninth chapters. Thus, upon the sounding of the first trumpet, the infliction falls upon the *earth;* and so it does upon the pouring out of the first vial. Upon the blast of the second trumpet, the *sea is* affected; and so it is upon the emptying of the second vial. When the third angel sounded, there fell a great star upon the rivers and fountains of water. So the third vial was poured out upon the rivers and fountains of water. When the fourth angel sounded, the sun was smitten; and the fourth angel poured out his vial upon the sun. The sounding of the sixth trumpet fell upon the great river Euphrates; and the sixth angel poured out his vial upon the same river.

These successive correspondences are certainly remarkable, and would seem to be designed. The reason of them may be this: The blasts of the several trumpets looked, as we have shown, to the overthrow of the vast Roman empire, whereas the plagues of the vials are designed for the destruction of *Papal Rome*—the beast, the Babylon, the antichrist of the New Testament. They are the successive blows under which the Papacy, in both its secular and spiritual dominion, is to come to an end. A part of these inflictions is still future, while some of them are passing, or past, and the application of them may perhaps be ascertained.

I agree with many distinguished commentators in referring several of the vials to events connected with the first French revolution. Nor is this to be wondered at, when we consider the intimate vital connection which has subsisted between France and the Papacy for the last thousand years. It was a king of France who first gave to the Pope his temporal dominions, and constituted him a king. And the French kings have ever held a peculiar connection with the Popes, sometimes coercing, and sometimes protecting, as the case might be. On the other hand, the monarch of France has long been styled by the Pope, 'His Most Christian

Majesty,' and 'the eldest son of the Church.' Let us then look to events preceding and following the revolution in France, as fulfilling the portents of some of these vials.

The First Vial.

'And the first angel went and poured out his vial upon the earth; and there fell a noisome and grievous sore upon the men which had the mark of the beast, and upon them that worshipped his image' (Rev. xvi. 2).

As noisome and grievous sores on the bodies of men indicate internal corruption—inflammation, tumours, and impurities of blood; so moral, political sores, and ulcers, prove the same in regard to a people. There must have been a preparation for such calamities in the minds and hearts of the people—in the inculcation of false principles, pernicious errors, and in the awakening by these means, of ruinous prejudices and passions. And this is precisely what had been going on in France for many years previous to the revolution. Infidelity and Atheism had been openly inculcated, until men had learned to scoff at everything respectable in morals and religion. The Bible had been thrown aside as a ruinous imposition, the God of the Bible had been rejected, and death was declared an eternal sleep. At the same time, there had been inculcated, under the specious names of

liberty and equality, the most radical and out-
rageous principles of social and political life. 'Away
with all distinctions between the high and the low,
the rich and the poor, the virtuous and the de-
graded, the honourable and the despised. All pre-
tensions of this sort must yield before the claims of
reason, and the rising light of the new philosophy.'

That such was the state of opinion and feeling
in France in the latter part of the last century, no
one acquainted with the history of the times can
doubt. The currents of social and political life had
all been corrupted, moral impurity throbbed through
the entire system, and no wonder the infection soon
made its appearance in noisome and grievous sores
and ulcers. What else was to be expected from such
a preparation? The odious and painful symbols of
the first vial here met a full significance.

The Second Vial.

'And the second angel poured out his vial upon
the sea; and it became as the blood of a dead man:
and every living soul died in the sea.'

As this vial was poured upon the sea, some interpreters are inclined to look for its fulfilment in
the naval defeats and losses of the French during
their revolutionary struggle. And these, certainly,
were numerous and crushing. It has been com-
puted that, during this bloody period, the French
lost two hundred ships of the line, between three

and four hundred frigates, and an incalculable number of smaller vessels.

But I am inclined to look for the significance of
the second vial in the revolution itself. We have
seen what preparation had long been making for it;
and in due time the vial of wrath came. At first,
under the National Assembly, the assault was chiefly
on the property of the citizens; but after the
establishment of the Convention,—when the nation
had become frantic at the alarm of foreign invasion,
which the king and the clergy were supposed to
favour,—the storm arose and prostrated every
thing. The Church and the throne went down together. From this time, the blasphemies, the blood,
and carnage of the revolution were quickly inaugurated; and the miseries which were endured
by that single nation, in the course of a few years,
transcend all description. The whole country
seemed to be turned into one great prison house,
the inhabitants to be converted into felons, and the
ordinary doom of man to be commuted for the
butchery of the sword and the guillotine. It
seemed for a time as if the knell of the whole
nation was tolled, and the world summoned to its
execution and funeral. Within the space of ten
years, not less than three million of human beings
are supposed to have perished in that one country.
Well may such an immolation be portended by

a sea of blood, in which every living creature dies.

The Third Vial.

'And the third angel poured out his vial upon the rivers and fountains of waters; and they became blood. And I heard the angel of the waters say, Thou art righteous, O Lord, which art, and wast, and shalt be, because Thou hast judged thus: for they have shed the blood of saints and prophets, and Thou hast given them blood to drink; for they are worthy. And I heard another out of the altar say, Even so, Lord God Almighty, true and righteous are Thy judgments' (Rev. xvi. 3–7).

We cannot mistake in applying this prediction to some Papal country abounding with streams and fountains, and where there had been much persecution. 'They have shed the blood of saints and prophets, and Thou hast given them blood to drink; for they are worthy.' The next material event, after the revolution in France, was the invasion of Italy, where Napoleon gained his first victories, and acquired his earliest fame. Here occurred the battles of Montenotte, Millesimo, and Dego; the passage of the bridge of Lodi, and the fall of Milan; the siege of Mantua, and the battle of Castiglione; the battles of Caldero, Arcola, and Rivola, and the fall of Venice. Most of these battles were on the branches of the Po—a country abound-

ing with rivers and streams, also a country long
reddened with the blood of martyrs.   Here the
persecutions of the Albigenses and Waldenses had
been perpretated, until the Alpine valleys literally
ran with blood.   The blood which was now given
them to drink was no more than a righteous retribution; and, from the blow which here fell upon
the Papal power, persecuting Rome has never
recovered.

The Fourth Vial.

'And the fourth angel poured out his vial upon
the sun; and power was given unto him to scorch
men with fire.   And men were scorched with great
heat, and blasphemed the name of God, which hath
power over these plagues: and they repented not
to give Him glory' (Rev. xvi. 8, 9).

Following out the train of remark already pursued, I cannot resist the conclusion, that the fourth
vial portended the wars of Napoleon in Germany
and Austria.   These followed immediately upon his
wars in Italy.   Indeed, one of the purposes for which
he invaded Italy was, to secure the Austrian posses-
sions there, and through them to reach Austria
itself.   These wars were crushing, and exceedingly
bloody.   They all tended to weaken the Papal
power, and ultimately to destroy it.   In their progress, as one well expresses it, ' Europe seemed to
be all on fire with musketry and artillery, present-

ing the blaze of a vast battle-field.' To the miser-
able inhabitants, it was as though the very sun in
the heavens had been commissioned to consume
and destroy them. Still they blasphemed the
name of God, and repented not to give Him the
glory.

The Fifth Vial.

'And the fifth angel poured out his vial upon the
seat of the beast; and his kingdom was full of darkness; and they gnawed their tongues for pain, and
blasphemed the God of heaven because of their
pains and their sores, and repented not of their
deeds' (Rev. xvi. 10, 11).

Though all the previous judgments had been
preparatory to the one here presented, the grand
object of the revolutionists had not as yet been
accomplished. The seat, the throne of the beast,
had not been reached. But now a vial of wrath is
poured directly upon it. The ecclesiastical states
of Italy, and the capital, were to be attacked. In
this delicate and responsible undertaking the French
Directory proceeded with more caution, and with a
greater show of moderation, than they were wont
to assume; still, their purpose was fixed, and they
firmly adhered to it. Early in the year 1799 Rome
was taken, and the tricolor flag floated on the summit
of the Capitol. The Pope was dragged from his
palace, his repositories were all ransacked and plun-

dered; even the rings were torn from his aged
fingers. He begged to be permitted to die where he
was; but he was told that he could die anywhere
else as well. He was first sent into Tuscany, then
to Leghorn, and thence was compelled to traverse
the Alps and Apennines on his way to France. But
he did not live to complete the journey. At Valence,
after an illness of ten days, Gregory XVI. expired, in
the 82d year of his age, and the 24th of his pontificate.

Meanwhile the French troops had commenced a
regular and systematic pillage of Rome. Not only
the churches and convents, but the palaces of the
nobility and the cardinals were laid waste. The
soldiers ransacked every quarter of the city, seized
the most valuable works of art, and carried away a
vast amount of treasure, which former conquerors
had spared.

It might seem that the Papal power was now
forever crushed. The deep hostility of the revolutionists, and their constant successes, apparently
looked to no other result. Events, however, soon
occurred to defeat such expectations; and as much
as this is indicated in the prediction before us. The
worshippers of the beast were not to be immediately
destroyed, but spared to renew their abominations.
'They gnawed their tongues for pain, and blasphemed the God of heaven, and repented not of
their deeds.'

Not long after the death of Gregory, and the sacking of Rome, some advantages were gained over the revolutionists, and the cardinals were emboldened to get together and elect a new Pontiff. Pius VII. was chosen on the 13th of March 1800. Napoleon made use of him for a time to further his ambitious designs, and Popery secured another respite.

The Sixth Vial.

' And the sixth angel poured out his vial upon the great river' Euphrates; and the water thereof was dried up, that the way of the kings of the East might be prepared.' 'And I saw three unclean spirits like frogs come out of the mouth of the dragon, and out of the mouth of the beast, and out of the mouth of the false prophet. For they are the spirits of devils, working miracles, which go forth unto the kings of the earth, and of the whole world, to gather them to the battle of that great day of God Almighty. Behold, I come as a thief. Blessed is he that watcheth, and keepeth his garments, lest he walk naked, and they see his shame. And He gathered them together into a place called in the Hebrew tongue Armageddon ' (Rev. xvi. 12–16).

The sixth trumpet we have before interpreted as opening the way for the Turks, to invade the Eastern Roman empire, and effect its overthrow. The sixth vial has reference, undoubtedly, to the same people;

but it seems to indicate, not their prevalence, but their removal, ' that the way of the kings of the East may be prepared.' Who these 'kings of the East' are, we do not know. Our hope is, that the work of evangelization will go on in the East—in Persia, China, India, Burmah—so that when the Turkish obstacle shall be removed, a Christian people may be prepared to come forward, and affiliate with their brethren of the West. Such an event would fulfil the portents of this vial, and we trust it may, ere long, be realized.

The Turkish empire, once so formidable to Christians, has long since passed its zenith, and is apparently verging to its end. Instead of being the terror of Christian Europe, it is now held up by the powers of Europe, in their jealousy one of another. For centuries there has been a gradual weakening of the Turkish power. Province after province has been dropping away, leaving it curtailed and feeble. Moldavia, Wallachia, Greece, Algiers, Morocco, and the other northern states of Africa, have revolted; and it holds but a nominal sway over Egypt; while Russia only waits its opportunity to strike a decisive blow, and put an end to the Turkish dominion for ever. And when this shall take place, a Christian East may be expected to come forward, as above hinted, and join hands and hearts with their brethren of the West.

And when the servants of Christ, in different parts of the world, become affiliated, and prepared to stand together, we may expect a mighty influence to be exerted against them. Who these unclean spirits are, in the shape of frogs, which are to come forth from the mouth of the dragon, the beast, and the false prophet, I pretend not to say. They may be the expiring *genii* of Paganism, Mahometanism, and of Popery, working together, as they have ever done, in opposition to the cause and kingdom of Christ. Or, they may be the hordes of Jesuit emissaries, who are now training for this very purpose, going forth to muster their armies for the final conflict. At any rate, there is to be such a conflict; and when the way is fully prepared for it, the seventh vial will be poured out.

The Seventh Vial.

'And the seventh angel poured out his vial into the air; and there came a great voice out of the temple of heaven, from the throne, saying, *It is done*. And there were voices, and thunders, and lightnings; and there was a great earthquake, such as was not since men were upon the earth, so mighty an earthquake, and so great. And the great city was divided into three parts, and the cities of the nations fell: and great Babylon came in remembrance before God, to give unto her the cup of the wine of the fierceness of his wrath. And every island fled away,

Y

and the mountains were not found. And there fell upon men a great hail out of heaven, every stone about the weight of a talent: and men blasphemed God because of the plague of the hail; for the plague thereof was exceeding great' (Rev. xvi. 17–21).

At the close of the sixth vial, the great conflict was fully inaugurated, and everything was in readiness for the final stroke. And now it falls. 'The seventh angel poured out his vial into the air; and there came a great voice out of the temple of heaven—from the very throne of God—saying, *It is done.'* The long agony is over. The dragon, the beast, the false prophet, and all those who bear their mark, or worship their image, are subdued, and the way is opened for the universal prevalence and triumph of the kingdom of Christ.

The voices, the thunders, the lightnings, and the earthquake denote the changes and revolutions connected with, and consequent upon, this glorious event. We can readily conceive that they must be very great,—such as the terrific symbols here employed do but feebly represent.

The great city here spoken of is, without doubt, the mystic Babylon,—the Papacy with all its adherents and dependents. The division of the city into three parts is probably spoken of as one of the means of its destruction; for we are immediately told, that 'great Babylon came in remembrance before God, to give unto her the cup of the wine of the fierceness of his wrath.'

Some of the symbols here employed, particularly the hail-stones, denote, not revolution, but destruction. There will be, there must be, in the crisis here spoken of, a terrible destruction of human life. Still, we perceive in this instance, as in several before introduced, that divine judgments, unless accompanied by the sanctifying Spirit, produce no good effect. They serve only to harden. 'Men blasphemed the name of God because of the plague of the hail; for the plague thereof was exceeding great.'

CHAPTER XV.

GOD'S JUDGMENT UPON THE GREAT WHORE.

REVELATION, CHAP. XVII.

A LTHOUGH the writer of the Revelation, or rather the Spirit which inspired him, had led us along at the end of the last chapter,—as he had before done in several instances,—to the close of the great conflict immediately preceding the millennium, he seems not to have been satisfied to leave the matter thus, but must give a new illustration of the grand enemy with which the Church had been called so long to contend, and of his final defeat and overthrow. 'And so,' says the writer, 'there came to me one of the seven angels which had the seven vials, and talked with me, saying, Come hither; I will show thee the judgment of the great whore that sitteth upon many waters, with whom the kings of the earth have committed fornication, and the inhabitants of the earth have been made drunk with the wine of her fornication' (Rev. xvii. 1–2).

This is a description of the whore by the angel; for John had not yet seen her. She is represented by the angel as having her seat upon many waters, as the literal Babylon was seated upon the Euphrates, and the literal Rome on the Tiber. These waters are subsequently interpreted as symbolizing the peoples, and multitudes, and nations, and tongues, over which the woman exerted her bewitching, intoxicating influence.

'So the angel carried me away in the spirit into the wilderness: and I saw a woman sit upon a scarlet-coloured beast, full of names of blasphemy, having seven heads and ten horns. And the woman was arrayed in purple and scarlet colour, and decked with gold, and precious stones, and pearls, having a golden cup in her hand full of abominations and filthiness of her fornication: and upon her forehead was a name written, MYSTERY, BABYLON THE GREAT, THE MOTHER OF HARLOTS AND ABOMINATIONS OF THE EARTH. And I saw the woman drunken with the blood of the saints, and with the blood of the martyrs of Jesus: and when I saw her, I wondered with great admiration. And the angel said unto me, Wherefore didst thou marvel? I will tell thee the mystery of the woman, and of the beast that carrieth her, which hath the seven heads and ten horns' (Rev. xvii. 3–7).

And so the angel proceeds to interpret the vision to the prophet, and to explain its significance. 'The beast that thou sawest was, and is not; and shall ascend out of the bottomless pit, and go into perdition: and they that dwell on the earth shall wonder, (whose names were not written in the book of life from the foundation of the world,) when they behold the beast that was, and is not, and yet is' (Rev. xvii. 8).

This is the same beast which John saw rise out of the sea in the beginning of the thirteenth chapter, and which we interpreted to signify Papal Rome, in its civil, secular, kingly authority. And if there could be any doubt as to the correctness of this interpretation before, we are confirmed in it by the interpretation of the angel here. 'Here is the mind that hath wisdom. The seven heads are seven mountains, on which the woman sitteth,'—referring to the seven hills on which Rome was built. 'And there are seven kings: five are fallen, and one is, and the other is not yet come; and when he cometh, he must continue a short space. And the beast that was, and is not, even he is the eighth, and is of the seven, and goeth into perdition. And the ten horns which thou sawest, are ten kings, which have received no kingdom as yet; but receive power as kings one hour with the beast. These have one mind, and shall give their power and strength unto the beast. These shall make war with the Lamb, and the Lamb shall overcome them; for he is Lord of lords and King of kings: and they that are with him, are called, and chosen, and faithful' (Rev. xvii. 9–14).

The seven kings here spoken of, as explained in a previous chapter, are the seven forms of government which had prevailed at Rome, viz., kings, consuls, dictators, decemvirs, military tribunes, and emperors,—the last of which governed Rome when the Apocalypse was written. Succeeding the fall of the emperors and the Gothic kings, Rome, with its environs, was reduced to a dukedom, subject to the exarch of Ravenna. This was the seventh form of government which, compared with what preceded and followed it, continued but 'a short space.' As to 'the beast that was and is not, which is the eighth and is of the seven,' there can be no difficulty in applying this to the Papacy, in its kingly authority. This was, in some sense, a new form of government, the eighth; and yet it is of the seven, —almost identical with two of them, viz., kings and emperors. It had the same central seat with the governments which preceded it,—that is, Rome; it extended over the same territory, and embraced, in its progress, the same nations. The ten horns of the beast are ten kingdoms, which had no existence at the time when this prophecy was written, but came up upon the overthrow and division of the Western Empire. They came into power, not *one* hour with the beast, but the *same hour* with him,—

which is a better rendering than that in our translation. These kingdoms existed at the same time with the beast, had the same mind with him, and gave their power and strength unto him. Under his influence 'they shall make war with the Lamb; but the Lamb shall overcome them; for He is Lord of lords, and King of kings.'

Such was the beast on which the whore was sitting,—Papal Rome, in its royal kingly authority. But what does the whore stand for? Whom does she represent? There can be as little doubt in this case as in the other. She represents the Papacy in its *spiritual* authority. She is identical with the second beast in the thirteenth chapter; and also with 'the false prophet,' who is so frequently associated with the beast, and is said to have 'wrought miracles before him, with which to deceive them which had the mark of the beast, and that worshipped his image' (chap. xix. 20). The design of this hideous and odious symbol—the woman—is to exhibit more fully than had yet been done, Papal Rome, in two aspects, viz., its *idolatries* and its *cruelties*. Idolatry is commonly spoken of in the Old Testament under the similitude of whoredom, adultery.[1] The idolatries of the Church of Rome are numberless. They are shamelessly open, and of long continuance. In the Iconoclast controversy

[1] See Jer. iii. 6–9 and xiii. 27; Ezek. xvi. 31–34.

of the eighth and ninth centuries, the bishops of Rome stood forth persistently as the advocates and defenders of image worship. And from those times to the present, they have persisted in their idolatries,—to the scandal of the Christian name with some other religions,—and will not give them up. In this respect she has fully justified the symbolism before us. She has proved herself to be the great whore which has corrupted the nations.

She also answers to the representation in the chapter before us in respect to the cruelties. She is ' drunk with the blood of the saints, and of the martyrs of Jesus.' There is no computing the murders of God's faithful witnesses, for which the Papal harlot is responsible. They are, I had almost said, numberless. If any one doubts the truth of this representation, let him consult the histories of the Albigenses and Waldenses, the Protestants of France, and the martyrs of the low countries. Let him go to the records of the Inquisition in Spain and Italy, and in every other country where this terrible court has been established. Rome may try to conceal these horrible tragedies, but she cannot cover them up. The blood of ten thousand martyrs is at this moment crying against her for vengeance. *Drunk with the blood of the saints and martyrs of Jesus—* this is the terrible indictment which stands against her in the court of heaven.

z

We have seen already that the ten horns of the beast, are the ten kingdoms into which the Western Empire was divided, which for a time gave their strength and power unto the beast, and with him made war with the Lamb. But it shall not be so always. The time will come when 'the ten horns shall hate the whore, and shall make her desolate and naked, and shall eat her flesh, and burn her with fire.' To a great extent, this period has come even now. Time was, when Germany, and England, and Scotland, and Holland, and Protestant Switzerland, were giving their strength to the beast and his paramour, and with them were united in making war upon the Lamb. But it is not so now. These nations have long since renounced this base allegiance, and enlisted themselves on the other side. And other nations are preparing to follow them. From present appearances, nothing is more likely than that Spain, and France, and Austria, and Italy, may, ere long, come to hate the whore as earnestly as they had ever loved her, and will unite with the other European kingdoms to make her desolate, and to burn her with fire. We wait the issues of these great events with confidence and prayer.

CHAPTER XVI.

THE FALL OF THE MYSTICAL BABYLON.

GREAT LAMENTATION ON EARTH, AND GREAT REJOICING IN HEAVEN, ON ACCOUNT OF IT.

REVELATION, CHAP. XVIII.

WE have in this chapter a more full and formal annunciation of the fall of the mystical Babylon—the great Papal, persecuting power—than in any previous instance. In the 14th chapter, we heard an angel crying: 'Babylon is fallen, is fallen, that great city, because she made all nations drink of the wine of the wrath of her fornication.' But here the cry is more loudly and formally repeated, and the feelings of different characters, both on earth and in heaven, are particularly described.

'After these things I saw another angel come down from heaven, having great power; and the earth was lightened with his glory. And he cried mightily with a strong voice, saying, Babylon the great is fallen, is fallen, and is become the habitation of devils, and the hold of every foul spirit, and a cage of every unclean and hateful bird. For all nations have drunk of the wine of the wrath of her fornication, and the kings of the earth have committed fornication with her, and the merchants of the earth are waxed rich through the abundance of her delicacies.' The charge here is, that the whole earth, the Roman earth, has been corrupted, more or less, by her intercourse, her commerce, and her idolatries.

' And I heard another voice from heaven, saying, Come out of her, my people, that ye be not partakers of her sins, and that ye receive not of her plagues : for her sins have reached unto heaven, and God hath remembered her iniquities.

' Reward her even as she rewarded you, and double unto her double according to her works : in the cup which she hath filled, fill to her double.' This command is addressed to those people and nations which had been wronged and persecuted by her. And they are called upon to render her double for her sins ; not double what she deserves at the hands of God, but double what is usually inflicted by injured nations upon their oppressors.

' How much she hath glorified herself, and lived deliciously, so much torment and sorrow give her : for she saith in her heart, I sit a queen, and am no widow, and shall see no sorrow. Therefore shall her plagues come in one day, death, and mourning, and famine ; and she shall be utterly burned with fire : for strong is the Lord God who judgeth her' (Rev. xviii. 1–8).

Next comes the lament of the kings of the earth, and the merchants and ship-masters—her guilty confederates and traffickers—over the fall and ruin of this mighty city.

' And the kings of the earth, who have committed fornication and lived deliciously with her, shall bewail her, and lament for her, when they shall see the smoke of her burning, standing afar off for fear of her torment, saying, Alas, alas, that great city Babylon, that mighty city! for in one hour is thy judgment come.

' And the merchants of the earth shall weep and mourn over her; for no man buyeth their merchandise any more. . . . They shall stand afar off for the fear of her torment, weeping and wailing, and saying, Alas, alas! that great city, that was clothed in fine linen, and purple, and scarlet, and decked with gold, and precious stones, and pearls; for in one hour so great riches is come to nought.'

' And every ship-master, and as many as trade by sea, stood afar off and cried, when they saw the smoke of her burning, saying, What city is like unto this great city! And they cast dust on their heads, and cried, weeping and wailing, and saying, Alas, alas, that great city! wherein were made rich all that had ships in the sea, by reason of her costliness; for in one hour she is made desolate' (Rev. xviii. 9–19).

While the wicked of the earth are thus wailing and lamenting over the fall of this mighty and corrupting city, the heavens are called upon to lift up their voice in a very different strain: 'Rejoice over her, thou heaven, and ye holy apostles and prophets; for God hath avenged you on her' (Rev. xviii. 20).

The close of the chapter records the inevitable and utter ruin of this doomed city,—another name for Papal Rome,—with the causes which produced it. 'And a mighty angel took up a stone like a great millstone, and cast it into the sea, saying, Thus with violence shall that great city Babylon be thrown down, and shall be found no more at all. And the voice of harpers, and musicians, and of pipers, and trumpeters, shall be heard no more at all in thee: and no craftsman, of whatsoever craft he be, shall be found any more in thee; and the sound of a millstone shall be heard no more at all in thee; and the light of a candle shall shine no more at all in thee; and the voice of the bridegroom and of the bride shall be heard no more at all in thee: for thy merchants were the great men of the earth; for by thy sorceries were all nations deceived. And in her was found the blood of prophets, and of saints, and of all that were slain upon the earth' (Rev. xviii. 21–24).

CHAPTER XVII.

REJOICINGS IN HEAVEN OVER THE FALL OF BABYLON.

CHRIST'S LAST CONFLICT AND TRIUMPH BEFORE THE MILLENNIUM.

REVELATION, CHAP. XIX.

THIS chapter opens with a song of thanksgiving and praise to God, for the recent destruction of the grand enemy of His Church and people. 'And after these things I heard a great voice of much people in heaven, saying, Alleluia ; Salvation, and glory, and honour, and power be unto the Lord our God : for true and righteous are His judgments : for He hath judged the great whore, which did corrupt the earth with her fornication, and hath avenged the blood of His servants at her hand. And again they said, Alleluia! And her smoke rose up for ever and ever. And the four and twenty elders, and the four living creatures, fell down and worshipped God that sat on the throne, saying, Amen, Alleluia! And a voice came out of the throne, saying, Praise our God, all ye His servants, and ye that fear Him, both small and great. And I heard as it were the voice of a great multude, and as the voice of many waters, and as the voice of mighty thunderings, saying, Alleluia! for the Lord God omnipotent reigneth' (Rev. xix. 1–6).

This grand pæan of praise, in which all creatures in heaven seem to have united, being over, the revealing angel addresses John on another subject. 'Let us be glad and rejoice, and give honour to him: for the marriage of the Lamb is come, and his wife hath made herself ready. And to her was granted that she should be arrayed in fine linen, clean and white: for the fine linen is the righteousness of saints;' that is, it symbolises, sets forth, the righteousness of saints. 'And he saith unto me, Write, Blessed are they which are called unto the marriage supper of the Lamb.' And as if to confirm the glorious revelation here made, the angel saith farther unto John, 'These are the true sayings of God' (Rev. xix. 7–9).

The connection between Christ and His people is continually set forth in the Scriptures by that between the bridegroom and bride. He is His Church's bridegroom, and she his bride. But this endearing relation, though subsisting through all the previous ages of darkness and conflict, is now to be more publicly and solemnly celebrated. The Church is about to enter on the comparative purity and blessedness of the millennial state. She is to be arrayed, as never before, in a robe of righteousness—fine linen, clean and white. In view of what was so glorious and so near at hand, the angel had much reason to say, 'Blessed are they that are called unto the marriage supper of the Lamb.'

In prospect of such honours and blessedness for the Church, the Apostle seems to have been quite overcome. He did what he had never before attempted, except when he fell at the feet of the glorified Saviour (Rev. i. 17). He fell at the feet of the angel to worship him; perhaps thinking that he was the Saviour. But he was instantly and appropriately rebuked. 'See thou do it not: I am thy fellow servant, and of thy brethren that have the testimony of Jesus: Worship God' (Rev. xix. 10).

The angel's language here does not imply, as some have thought, that he was the glorified spirit of some ancient prophet or saint. He was undoubtedly an *angel*, as he is here called; and it is an honour to us that holy angels are willing to acknowledge themselves as our fellow servants, and as brethren to all those who have the testimony of Jesus. 'For,' adds the angel, in a very pregnant passage, 'the testimony of Jesus is the spirit of prophecy.' As much as to say, 'Every true prophet or preacher—every one who has the true spirit of prophecy, *will testify of Jesus.* This will be his chief and central topic. A test here of the genuine prophet's commission.

2 A

A new and glorious vision is now presented to the view of the admiring Apostle. As, on the opening of the first seal, he 'saw a white horse, and he that sat on him had a bow, and a crown was given unto him, and he went forth conquering and to conquer;' so here, in the closing vision of the great conflict, the same divine personage is presented again. 'I saw heaven opened, and behold a white horse; and he that sat upon him was called Faithful and True; and in righteousness he doth judge and make war. His eyes were as a flame of fire, and on his head were many crowns; and he had a name written that no man knew but himself; and he was clothed in a vesture dipped in blood: and his name is called The Word of God. And the armies which were in heaven followed him upon white horses, clothed in fine linen, white and clean. And out of his mouth goeth a sharp sword, that with it he should smite the nations: and he shall rule them with a rod of iron : and he treadeth the wine-press of the fierceness and wrath of Almighty God. And he hath on his vesture and on his thigh a name written, KING OF KINGS, AND LORD OF LORDS' (Rev. xix. 11–16).

Such was the appearance and the retinue of the great Son of God, going forth to the last conflict previous to the commencement of His millennial kingdom. The issue of the conflict may be gathered from what follows: ' And I saw an angel standing in the sun ; and he cried with a loud voice, saying to all the fowls that fly in the midst of heaven, Come and gather yourselves together unto the supper of the great God ; that ye may eat the flesh of kings, and the flesh of captains, and the flesh of mighty men, and the flesh of horses, and of them that sit on them, and the flesh of all men, both free and bond, both small and great. And I saw the beast, and the kings of the earth, and their armies, gathered together to make war against him that sat on the horse, and against his army. And the beast was taken, and with him the false prophet that wrought miracles before him, with which he deceived them that had received the mark of the beast, and them that worshipped his image. These both were cast alive into a lake of fire burning with brimstone. And the remnant were slain with the sword of him that sat upon the horse, which sword proceedeth out of his mouth: and all the fowls were filled with their flesh' (Rev. xix. 17–21).

My first remark in regard to these Scriptures is, that they do not stand alone in describing the closing conflict before the millennium. They have been preceded by several others ; and yet the accounts are not repetitions. The symbolism is different, and they present different phases or aspects of the same closing scene. Thus the seventh seal,—including, as it does, the seven trumpets,— runs down to the millennium: For when the seventh angel had sounded, 'there were great voices in heaven, saying, The kingdoms of this world have become the kingdoms of our Lord and of His Christ, and He shall reign for ever and ever' (chap. xi. 15). The two witnesses continued their testimony to the close of the twelve hundred and sixty years (chap. xi. 3). And the same may be said of the hiding of the mystical woman in the wilderness (chap. xii. 6), and the tyranny of the Popish beasts (chap. xiii. 5). Both these continued to the end of the twelve hundred and sixty years, and with the closing up of that period, the millennium commences. So the vintage of the earth described in the fourteenth chapter, and the pouring out the seventh vial, in the sixteenth, and the fall of Babylon in the eighteenth,—these all present the close of the final conflict—the same that is predicted in the nineteenth chapter. As I have said before, none of these predictions reach into the millennium, or go beyond it. They all terminate at the same point, presenting different views of the long struggle of the Church with its mortal enemies, and of the closing conflict, which brings an abiding peace. I deem this a very important position to be taken in interpreting the Apocalypse—one which tends to simplify its interpretation and make it plain.

It is a common impression among Christians that, previous to the millennium, all the inhabitants of the earth are to be converted. But the Scriptures before us, and other Scriptures referring to the same event, teach a different doctrine. In bringing in the millennial period, vast numbers of the incorrigible enemies of God and His people will be cut off.

In preparation for the millennium, the gospel will be universally diffused. It will be preached for a witness to all nations. Those who embrace it, and enrol themselves among the servants of Christ, will be safe. But those who persist in rejecting it, and in opposing the triumphs of the Son of God, will be taken out of the way. As much as this is indicated in a variety of Scriptures. Thus, in Daniel, the power denoted by the beast and the little horn, is represented, not as converted, but terribly destroyed. 'I beheld even till the beast was slain, and his body given to the burning flame' (Dan. vii. 11). And so of Paul's 'man of sin,' and 'son of perdition,' it is said, 'whom the Lord shall consume with the breath of His mouth, and destroy with the brightness of His coming' (2 Thess. ii. 8). And the same view is continually presented in the Revelation. There is the mustering of the hosts of the wicked, and the gathering of them together at Armageddon to the battle of the great day of God Almighty (chap.

xvi.). There is the account of the last vintage, when the wicked of the earth are reaped, and cast together 'into the great winepress of the wrath of God;' and when 'the winepress was trodden without the city, blood came out of the winepress, even unto the horses' bridles, for the space of one thousand six hundred furlongs' (chap. xiv. 20). And so in the closing verses of the nineteenth chapter: 'All the fowls of heaven are summoned together unto the supper of the great God, that they may eat the flesh of kings, and the flesh of captains, and the flesh of mighty men, and the flesh of horses, and of them that sit on them, and the flesh of all men, both free and bond, both small and great.' Here certainly is a symbolic representation of great and terrible destruction immediately preceding the introduction of the millennium. What else can we make of it?

There is indeed an intimation,—and I rejoice to record it,—that some of those who persist in their hostility to Christ almost to the last, are to be finally saved. 'The remnant were slain with the sword of him that sat upon the horse, which sword proceeded out of his mouth.' The sword proceeding out of the mouth of Christ I understand to be 'the sword of the Spirit, which is the Word of God.' A remnant of those who had enlisted in opposition to the Son of God, and had persisted in their opposition almost to the last, are at length delivered. Their enmity is slain by the sharp sword of the Spirit proceeding out of the mouth of Christ; and when all with whom they had been associated are cut off, and their bodies given to the vultures for a prey, they are saved so as by fire.

CHAPTER XVIII.

THE MILLENNIUM.

THE GENERAL RESURRECTION AND JUDGMENT, AND THE FINAL DESTRUCTION OF THE WICKED.

REVELATION, CHAP. XX.

THE beast and the false prophet, with all those that worshipped their image and followed in their train, are now cut off. They have been cast alive into the lake of fire. Only one enemy remains; and he,—the instigator of all that the Church has ever suffered,—is the most formidable of all. This is the old dragon,—who persecuted the woman, and endeavoured to slay her son,—who gave to the beast 'his power, his seat, and his great authority.' But his time has come, at length. His 'judgment lingereth not, and his damnation slumbereth not.'

'I saw an angel come down from heaven, having the key of the bottomless pit, and a great chain in his hand. And he laid hold on the dragon, that old serpent, which is the Devil and Satan, and bound him a thousand years, and cast him into the bottomless pit, and shut him up, and set a seal upon him, that he should deceive the nations no more, till the thousand years should be fulfilled: and after that he must be loosed a little season' (Rev. xx. 1–3).

And thus the millennium—that season of rest and peace which had been so long predicted by the prophets—is ushered in. That old serpent, who had been the fomentor of all wickedness, from the first apostacy, to the period of which we speak, is seized and bound, and effectually confined.

The description here is indeed symbolical; but as much as this is certainly intended by it, that the influence of Satan, which has so long been predominant in the earth, is now to be restrained. He is no longer to 'go about like a roaring lion, seeking whom he may devour.' He is confined in his prison, and shall go out 'to deceive the nations no more, until the thousand years shall be fulfilled.'

And what is to follow his confinement? What is to be the state of things on the earth?

'And I saw thrones, and they sat upon them, and judgment was given unto them: and I saw the souls of them that were beheaded for the witness of Jesus, and for the word of God, and which had not worshipped the beast, neither his image, neither had received his mark upon their foreheads, or on their hands; and they lived and reigned with Christ a thousand years. But the rest of the dead lived not again until the thousand years were finished. This is the first resurrection. Blessed and holy is he that hath part in the first resurrection : on such the second death hath no power; but they shall be priests of God and of Christ, and shall reign with Him a thousand years' (Rev. xx. 4—6).

It is to be carefully noted that these verses, like those preceding them, are entirely symbolical. Interpreters not a few have blundered here. The verses just quoted they have interpreted literally; and hence all their fancies respecting a literal, millennial resurrection of the saints, and the personal reign of Christ with them on the earth. Interpreted symbolically, as it must be, like the rest of the chapter, the passage gives no countenance to any such delusions: ' And I saw thrones, and they sat upon them. and I saw the souls of them that were beheaded for the witness of Jesus, and for the word of God, and which had not worshipped the beast, neither his image; and they lived and reigned with Christ a thousand years.' It will be observed that here is a prediction of the resurrection, not of all the holy dead which had left the world previous to the millennium, but only of the *martyrs* who had ' been beheaded for the witness of Jesus, and for the word of God.' Nor are the bodies even of these to be raised, but only their souls.

Stripped of its symbolical dress, and interpreted. as it must be, this passage merely sets forth the state of the world during the millennial period.

Christ is to reign, not bodily, but spiritually, on the earth, and His people are to reign spiritually with Him. The martyrs are to be raised in *spirit*, not in the body. The spirit of the martyrs is to be predominant. In other words, the millennium is to be a time of pre-eminent holiness. The inhabitants of the world generally are to be as holy as the martyrs. This resurrection and prevalence of the martyr spirit is the first resurrection. Blessed and holy are they who have part in such a resurrection. Over them, of course, the second death has no power, but they—in successive generations—shall live and spiritually reign with Christ a thousand years. But the rest of the dead—the unholy dead —are not to live again in spirit; in other words, their spirit is not to prevail until the thousand years are finished.

Such I conceive to be the meaning of this much disputed passage. And thus interpreted, is it not full of glorious meaning—more glorious than any literal interpretation could be? What can be better than a universal and spiritual reign with Christ—a time of pre-eminent knowledge and holiness? The earth will then be full of the knowledge and love of God, as the waters fill the channels of the deep. There will no longer be any occasion for one to say to another, Know the Lord, because all shall know Him, from the least even unto the greatest.

196 OF THE APOCALYPSE EXPLAINED:

As to the duration of the millennium, it is repeatedly promised that it shall continue a thousand years. Is this to be understood literally; or, is it to be understood—as numbers denoting time sometimes are in prophetical language—tropically, a day standing for a year?

I have before shown that, in interpreting the prophecies, we are at liberty—where the connection and sense require it (as they certainly do in many instances), to substitute a year for a day. But does the connection or sense require any such substitution here? I cannot say that they do. I incline rather to the opinion that they require a literal interpretation. If, in estimating the duration of the millennium, we are to substitute a year for a day, then this season of rest and peace will continue 360,000 years. But in this period the earth would be entirely filled with inhabitants,—so filled, according to some computations, as not to allow a square foot to each individual. Besides, there is to be a defection at the close of the millennium; and if this is to continue 360,000 years, such an event is scarcely conceivable. My belief therefore is, that what we call the millennium will be a literal *millennium*,—a thousand years.

The Last Defection and its Issue.

'And when the thousand years are expired, Satan shall be loosed out of his prison, and shall go out to deceive the nations that are in the four quarters of the earth, Gog and Magog, to gather them together to battle: the number of whom is as the sand of the sea. And they went up on the breadth of the earth, and compassed the camp of the saints about, and the beloved city: and fire came down from God out of heaven, and devoured them. And the devil that deceived them was cast into the lake of fire and brimstone, where the beast and the false prophet are, and shall be tormented day and night for ever and ever' (Rev. xx. 7–10).

Second-Advent interpreters have found it difficult to account for the great defection at the close of the millennium; but with sober views as to the state of things during the millennium, this event, though most unreasonable in itself, is not altogether unaccountable.

It must be borne in mind that the millennium will not change the natures of men. Children will be born then, as they are now, depraved creatures, and will need, as we do, to be born again, in order to see the kingdom of God. To be sure—in the absence of Satanic temptations, and under the influence of the best means, and in the midst of special outpourings of the Holy Spirit—they will be generally and early converted. They will also be deeply sanctified. Perhaps not every individual on the face of the earth at that period will be holy; but this will be true of mankind generally. Religion will predominate over all other interests. ' The kingdom, and dominion, and greatness of the kingdom under the whole heaven, will be given to the people of the saints of the Most High.' And this state of things will continue, generation after generation, for a thousand years.

But as this period draws to a close, Satan will be let loose, and his seductions will begin to prevail. At the same time, Divine influences will be comparatively withdrawn. God permits this state of things that he may show, in one more example, what sin and Satan are, and (if left to themselves) what they will do. A generation will soon come up, haters of God, despisers of His truth, and the enemies of His people. They will be restive under the restraints of the gospel, and will resolve to throw them off. ' We have been curbed and hampered by this religion long enough. The world must have more liberty. Let us break His bands asunder, and cast away His cords from us.'

Knowing what human nature is, when exposed to new temptations and free from spiritual restraints, we can easily conceive how this thing will work. A great party will soon be formed in opposition to Christ and His people, and every means will be resorted to, to enlist the world against the gospel. If other methods fail, a resort at length may be had to arms. A vast army may be gathered, Gog and Magog, and all the wicked of every name. They will be in number as the sand of the sea, and will compass the camp of the saints about, and the beloved city.

But their end is come. They shall proceed no farther. The saints will not be required to lift a weapon or to strike a blow in this fearful conflict. Suddenly, 'fire comes down from God out of heaven,'—perhaps the fires of the last conflagration,—and consumes them all. And the devil that deceived them is cast into the lake of fire and brimstone, where the beast and the false prophet are, and shall be tormented day and night for ever and ever.

The Last Judgment and Final Destruction of the Wicked.

'And I saw a great white throne, and Him that sat on it, from whose face the earth and the heaven fled away; and there was found no place for them. And I saw the dead, small and great, stand before God; and the books were opened: and another book was opened which is the book of life: and the dead were judged out of those things which were written in the books, according to their works. And the sea gave up the dead which were in it; and death and hell delivered up the dead which were in them: and they were judged every man according to their works. And death and hell were cast into the lake of fire. This is the second death. And whosoever was not found written in the book of life was cast into the lake of fire' (Rev. xx. 11–15).

The account here given of the last judgment is very like to that in other parts of the New Testament,—more especially to our Saviour's account of it in Mat. xxv. 31–46. It comes in, in the right place, and is one of the incontrovertible proof-texts going to establish the fact of such a scene. The fleeing away of earth and heaven before the face of the Judge refers to the general conflagration of the last day, when 'the heavens shall pass away with a great noise, the elements shall melt with fervent heat, the earth also and the works that are therein shall be burned up' (2 Pet. iii. 10).

The general resurrection is noted in the following passage: 'The sea gave up the dead which were in it, and death and hell gave up the dead which were in them.' Death and hell are here personified, denoting the whole realm of death and the grave. The original word, ἅδης, here translated hell, is used to signify the grave, as it often does in other parts of the Bible. The meaning is, that all the dead, whether on the earth, or under it, or in the sea, are raised and brought together to the judgment. And as there will be no more temporal dissolution, death and the grave are represented as destroyed. They are cast into the lake of fire.

Among the books here spoken of is the book of God's remembrance, in which is recorded every act of every individual of the human race, and out of which every one is to be judged according to his works. 'Who will bring every work into judgment, with every secret thing, whether it be good, or whether it be evil' (Ecc. xii. 14).

In the book of life are securely recorded the names of all God's people. 'And whosoever was not found written in the book of life was cast into the lake of fire' (Rev. xx. 15). Such is to be the end of all the wicked of the earth. 'Who shall be punished with everlasting destruction from the presence of the Lord, and from the glory of His power (2 Thess. i. 9).

CHAPTER XIX.

GLORIOUS DESTINATION OF THE RIGHTEOUS — SYM-
BOLICAL REPRESENTATION OF THE CHURCH IN
HEAVEN — CONCLUSION.

REVELATION, CHAPS. XXI., XXII.

THE multitude of the wicked being thus dis-
posed of, our attention is next called to the
final destination of the righteous : 'I saw a new
heaven and a new earth ; for the first heaven and
the first earth were passed away; and there was
no more sea' (Rev. xxi. 1).

The heaven here spoken of was the visible
heaven—the firmament.   The first heaven and
earth have passed away, being consumed in the
fires of the general conflagration.   In place of them,
John saw a new heaven and a new earth.   So
Peter concludes his account of the destruction of
the world by saying, 'We look for new heavens
and a new earth, wherein dwelleth righteousness'
(2 Pet. iii. 13).   Whether this new earth is to be
reconstructed from the materials of the former
earth, I pretend not to say.   The phrase may be

used as a symbol to denote the final, glorious abode
of God's people.

John is next shown the glories of the heavenly
Church, under the symbol of a holy and beautiful
city, coming down from God out of heaven, and
destined to rest, apparently, on the new earth.

'And I John saw the holy city, new Jerusalem,
coming down from God out of heaven, prepared as
a bride adorned for her husband. And I heard a
great voice out of heaven,'—probably the voice of
an angel,—'saying, Behold, the tabernacle of God
is with men, and He will dwell with them,'—in His
tabernacle—'and they shall be His people, and God
himself shall be with them, and be their God. And
God shall wipe away all tears from their eyes; and
there shall be no more death, neither sorrow, nor
crying, neither shall there be any more pain: for
the former things are passed away. 'And He
that sat upon the throne,' — the Messiah, —
'said, Behold, I make all things new,'—a new
heaven and a new earth, and a new order of things
to correspond with that creation. 'And He said
unto me, Write,'—record what you see and hear,—
'for these words are true and faithful. And He said
unto me, It is done.' The great work of redemption
is accomplished; the drama of this world's history
is closed; the redeemed are all gathered in; the
wicked are cut off; truth and holiness are trium-

phant; and all things are prepared for the eternal state. 'I am Alpha and Omega, the beginning and the end: I will give unto him that is athirst of the fountain of the water of life freely. He that over-cometh shall inherit all things; and I will be his God, and he shall be my son. But the fearful, and unbelieving, and the abominable, and murderers, and whoremongers, and sorcerers, and idolaters, and all liars, shall have their part in the lake which burneth with fire and brimstone: which is the second death' (Rev. xxi. 6–8).

As yet, John had got but a glimpse of the holy city—the new Jerusalem—the representative of the glorified Church; but now he is to be favoured with a particular view of it; accordingly; 'There came unto me one of the seven angels which had the seven vials full of the seven last plagues, and talked with me, saying, Come hither, I will shew thee the bride, the Lamb's wife. And he carried me away in the spirit'—not bodily—' to a great and high moun-tain,'—where the best view possible could be had,—' and shewed me that great city, the holy Jerusa-lem, descending out of heaven from God, having the glory of God; and her light was like unto a stone most precious, even like a jasper-stone, clear as crystal; and had a wall great and high, and had twelve gates, and at the gates twelve angels, and names written thereon, which are the names of the twelve tribes of the children of Israel : on the east, three gates; on the north, three gates; on the south, three gates; and on the west, three gates. And the wall of the city had twelve foundations' —foundation-stones—'and in them the names of the twelves apostles of the Lamb' (Rev. xxi. 9–14).

There can be no stronger proof of the unity, the identity, of God's Church, under both dispensations, than is here furnished. We have here a most splendid city—the bride, the Lamb's wife—the emblem and representative of the glorified Church. On the twelve gates of the city are inscribed the names of the *twelve tribes of the children of Israel*, and on the twelve foundation-stones the names of the *twelve apostles of the Lamb.* 'Built upon the foundation of the *apostles* and *prophets,* Jesus Christ himself being the chief corner stone' (Eph. ii. 20).

'And he'—the angel—'that talked with me had a golden reed to measure the city, and the gates thereof, and the wall thereof. And the city lieth four square, and the length is as large as the breadth. And he measured the city with the reed, twelve thousand furlongs,'—1500 miles in circumference— 375 miles on each side. 'The length, and the breadth, and the height of it are equal.' What a city! The Church of the first born, whose names are written in heaven! (Rev. xxi. 15, 16).

' And he measured the wall thereof, an hundred
and forty and four cubits, according to the measure
of a man ; that is, of the angel.'   The wall was of a
moderate height, compared with the extent of the
city.   ' And the building of the wall of it was of
jasper; and the city was pure gold, like unto clear
glass.   And the foundations of the wall of the city
were garnished with all manner of precious stones.'
(We omit the names of the gems which went into the
foundations.)   'And the twelve gates were twelve
pearls ; every several gate was of one pearl : and the
street of the city was pure gold, as it were trans-
parent glass.   And I saw no temple therein : for the
Lord God Almighty and the Lamb are the temple
of it.'   Every place in the city is a temple,—a place
of worship.   ' And the city had no need of the sun,
neither of the moon, to shine in it ; for the glory of
God did lighten it, and the Lamb is the light
thereof.   And the nations of them which are saved
shall walk in the light of it : and the kings of the
earth '—that are saved—' do bring their glory and
honour into it,'—everything which they regard as
constituting to their glory, laying it all down at the
feet of the Saviour, and consecrating and devoting
it all to His service.   ' And the gates of it shall not
be shut at all by day ; for there shall be no night
there.   And they shall bring the glory and honour
of the nations into it.   And there shall in no

wise enter into it anything that defileth, neither whatsoever worketh abomination, or maketh a lie; but they which are written in the Lamb's book of life' (Rev. xxi. 17–27).

'And he shewed me a pure river of water of life, clear as crystal, proceeding out of the throne of God and of the Lamb. In the midst of the street of it,'—the city—'and on either side of the river, was there the tree of life, which bare twelve manner of fruits, and yielded her fruit every month: and the leaves of the tree were for the healing of the nations' (Rev. xxii. 1, 2).

The imagery here is borrowed from the garden of Eden, and, more closely, from the mystical city described by Ezekiel, in some of the last chapters of his prophecy.[1] In each of them is a river, and in each is the tree of life, 'the fruit whereof,' says Ezekiel, 'shall be for meat, and the leaf thereof for medicine,'—or as John has it,— 'for the healing of the nations.'—(*See* Ezek. xlvii. 12.)

'And there shall be no more curse: but the throne of God and the Lamb shall be in it; and His servants shall serve Him: and they shall see His face; and His name shall be in their foreheads. And there shall be no night there; and they need no candle, neither light of the sun; for the Lord

[1] See Appendix.

God giveth them light: and they shall reign for
ever and ever'[1] (Rev. xxii. 3–5).

What follows may be regarded as the epilogue
or conclusion of this wonderful book. 'And he'—
the angel—'said unto me, These sayings are faithful and true: and the Lord God of the holy prophets sent His angel to shew unto His servants
the things which must shortly be done.' And then,
speaking in the name of Christ, or quoting a declaration of Christ, the angel goes on to say: 'Behold,
I come quickly: blessed is he that keepeth the sayings of the prophecy of this book' (Rev. xxii. 6, 7).

Regarding these as the words of Christ, and the
speaker as none other than Christ himself, John is
about to worship him: 'And I John saw these
things and heard them. And when I had heard and
seen, I fell down to worship before the feet of the
angel which shewed me these things. Then saith
he unto me, See thou do it not; for I am thy fellow
servant, and of thy brethren the prophets, and of
them which keep the sayings of this book: worship
God' (Rev. xxii. 8, 9).

The language here does not imply that the

---

[1] We are not to regard the city here described as the *residence* of
God's glorified Church, but rather as a symbol of the Church itself.
The Church is often represented in Scripture as a city, a building.
We believe there is such a place as heaven. ' I go to prepare a *place*
for you.' But where this locality is, and what its structure, form, or
extent, we have no knowledge.

speaker was the spirit of some old prophet. He was an angel—one of the seven angels who inflicted the seven last plagues. Still, he was a prophet like John, and a fellow servant with him of the same God and Saviour.

'Then saith he'—the angel—'unto me, Seal not the sayings of the prophecy of this book; for the time is at hand.' Seal them not up, as words not lawful to be uttered, but publish them abroad for a comfort to thy brethren, and a warning to the wicked. 'He that is unjust, let him be unjust still; and he which is filthy, let him be filthy still; and he that is righteous, let him be righteous still; and he that is holy, let him be holy still.' As much as to say, There will be no more changes. Probation is ended. The work of redemption is closed. The wicked have gone away into the lake of fire. The righteous have been received to everlasting habitations. 'He that is unjust, let him be unjust still; and he that is holy, let him be holy still' (Rev. xxii. 10, 11).

Personating Christ, as he was instructed to do, the angel continues: 'Behold I come quickly, and my reward is with me, to give to every man according as his work shall be. I am Alpha and Omega, the beginning and the end, the first and the last. Blessed are they that do His commandments, that they may have a right to the tree of life, and may

enter in through the gates into the city. For without'—without the heavenly city, in the regions of
darkness and woe—'are dogs, and sorcerers, and
whoremongers, and murderers, and idolators, and
whosoever loveth and maketh a lie' (Rev. xxii.
12–15).

All that are without are not only sufferers, but
sinners. And they will sin and suffer for ever.
They repent not of their evil deeds.

The Lord Jesus, who had spoken by His angel,
now speaks in His own person: 'I Jesus have sent
mine angel to testify unto you these things in the
Churches. I am the root and the offspring of David,
and the bright and morning star. And the Spirit and
the bride say, Come. And let him that heareth say,
Come. And let him that is athirst come. And whosoever will, let him take the water of life freely'
(Rev. xxii. 16–17).

The closing words of the book seem to be those
of John himself. 'I testify unto every man that
heareth the words of the prophecy of this book, If
any man shall add unto these things, God shall add
unto him the plagues that are written in this book:
And if any man shall take away from the words of
the book of this prophecy, God shall take away his
part out of the book of life, and out of the holy city,
and from the things which are written in this book.
He which testifieth these things'—*i.e.*, Christ—

' saith, Surely I come quickly : Amen.'   And to this
the writer responds, ' Even so, come, Lord Jesus.
The grace of our Lord Jesus Christ be with you all,
Amen' (Rev. xxii. 18–21).

Thus sweetly and delightfully does this blessed
book close, bearing as it were the music of heaven
upon the listening ear. O thou Root and Offspring
of David; thou Bright and Morning Star: condescend to guide us through the remaining darkness
of our pilgrimage, till we are ushered into the sun-
light of eternal day !

CHAPTER XX. ·

NO inconsiderable part of the book of Revelation consists of songs—songs of praise to God and the Lamb. And it is to be remembered that these are all of them heavenly songs,—full of earnestness, and glowing with the spirit of heaven,— sung on different occasions by the rapt choirs above.

We have a few specimens of heavenly songs— and but a few—in other parts of the Bible. There is the Song of the Seraphim, in the sixth chapter of Isaiah: 'Holy, holy, holy is the Lord of hosts, the whole earth is full of His glory.' There is the Song of the Angels at the birth of Christ; 'Glory to God in the highest; peace on earth and good will towards men.' But in the Revelation we have many such songs; and it seems important that they should receive a more particular consideration than we have been able to give them in the foregoing chapters.

There is, in the first place, the Song of the living creatures, or cherubim, on our first introduction to them. 'They rest not day and night saying, Holy, holy, holy, Lord God Almighty, which was, and is, and is to come.' This is very like the song of the seraphim in Isaiah,—one continual ascription of holiness to the Lord. In connection with this, the four and twenty elders present themselves before God, in a posture of the utmost humility and reverence, falling down in His presence, casting their crowns at His feet, and say-ing, 'Thou art worthy, O Lord, to receive glory, and honour, and power; for Thou hast created all things, and for Thy pleasure they are and were created' (Rev. iv. 8–11).

This is equivalent to the saying of Solomon, 'The Lord hath made all things for Himself' (Prov. xvi. 4)—*i.e.* to promote His glory, and contribute to His praise. This song of the elders and the cherubim was sung on no particular occasion, and may be regarded as a specimen of their daily, con-tinual worship.

Next, we have the new Song, sung by the elders and the cherubim, when the Lamb came for-ward and took the book out of the hand of Him that sat upon the throne. 'And when he had taken the book, the four living creatures and the four and twenty elders fell down before the Lamb, having every one of them harps and golden vials full of odours'—incense—'which are,' or which symbolize, 'the prayers of saints. And they sung a new song, saying, Thou art worthy to take the book, and to open the seals thereof: for thou wast slain, and hast redeemed us to God by Thy blood out of every kindred, and tongue, and people, and nation; and hast made us unto our God kings and priests: and we shall reign on the earth.'

From the very purport of this song, it could be sung only by the redeemed in heaven. Angels could not sing, ' Who hath loved us and washed us from our sins in His own blood.' Accordingly, the great choir of angels stand back in silence, while this part of the heavenly service is performed. But then a chorus was added,—one of the grandest that was ever sung on earth or in heaven, in which all the celestials can unite. ' I beheld, and I heard the voice of many angels round about the throne, and the living creatures, and the elders: and the number of them was ten thousand times ten thousand, and thousands of thousands, saying with a loud voice, Worthy is the Lamb that was slain to receive power, and riches, and wisdom, and strength, and honour, and glory, and blessing. And every creature which is in heaven, and on the earth, and under the earth, and such as are in the sea, and all that are in them, heard I saying, Blessing, and honour, and glory, and power, be unto Him that sitteth upon the throne, and unto the Lamb, for ever and ever' (Rev. v. 11–13).

There is not a passage in the Bible which gives us a nobler, grander, conception of heaven than this. The vast multitude in heaven, cherubim and seraphim, angels and glorified saints, ten thousand times ten thousand, and thousands of thousands, all uniting in one sublime chorus: 'Blessing, and honour, and glory, and power, be unto Him that sitteth on the throne, and unto the Lamb, for ever and ever!'

We have a similar Song of praise upon the sealing of the servants of God in their foreheads. Here, as in the last instance, the ransomed ones commence the strain, and are followed, in grand chorus, by the angels, 'I beheld, and, lo, a great multitude, which no man could number, of all nations, and kindreds, and people, and tongues, stood before the throne, and before the Lamb, clothed with white robes, and palms in their hands; and they cried with a loud voice, saying, Salvation to our God which sitteth upon the throne, and unto the Lamb. And all the angels stood round about the throne, and about the elders and the four living creatures, and fell before the throne on their faces, and worshipped God, saying, Amen: Blessing, and glory, and wisdom, and thanksgiving, and honour, and power, and might, be unto our God for ever, Amen' (Rev. vii. 9–12).

The next Song in heaven is sung by the elders

alone, on the sounding of the seventh trumpet, when the inspiring annunciation was made: 'The kingdoms of this world have become the kingdoms of our Lord and of His Christ, and He shall reign for ever and ever. And the four and twenty elders, which sat before God on their seats, fell upon their faces and worshipped God, saying, We give thee thanks, O Lord God Almighty, which art, and wast, and art to come; because thou hast taken to thee thy great power, and hast reigned. And the nations were angry, and thy wrath is come, and the time of the dead, that they should be judged, and that thou shouldst give reward unto thy servants the prophets, and to the saints, and them that fear Thy name, small and great; and shouldst destroy them which destroy the earth' (Rev. xi. 15, 16).

This is, in the first place, a song of thanksgiving to God for His righteous government over the world, and care of His people. It also celebrates God's glorious justice, in giving reward unto His servants, and destroying them that had destroyed the earth.

We have next a triumphal Song, sung, apparently, by the entire host of heaven, on the victory of Michael over the dragon. 'Now is come salvation, and strength, and the kingdom of our God, and the power of his Christ; for the accuser of our

brethren is cast down, which accused them before
our God day and night. And they overcame him
by the blood of the Lamb, and by the word of their
testimony; and they loved not their lives unto the
death. Therefore rejoice, ye heavens, and ye that
dwell in them. Woe to the inhabiters of the
earth, and of the sea! for the devil is come down
unto you, having great wrath, because he knoweth
that he hath but a short time' (Rev. xii. 10–12).

Satan is here spoken of as the accuser of God's
people—accusing them of falls, weaknesses, incon-
sistencies, imperfections. And how have they answered these charges, and refuted their merciless
adversary? Not by denying them, or excusing
them, or by off-setting against them their own
good deeds; no, but 'by the blood of the Lamb.'
There is no other way in which Satan's accusation
can ever be met and vanquished.

The next Song of which we hear in heaven is
that of the 144,000, who have their Father's name
written on their foreheads. It is sung by them,
and by them only. 'I heard a voice from heaven,
as the voice of many waters, and as the voice of a
great thunder: and I heard the voice of harpers
harping with their harps: and they sung as it
were a new song before the throne, and before the
four living creatures, and the elders; and no man
could learn that song but the hundred and forty

and four thousand, which were redeemed from the earth' (Rev. xiv. 2, 3).

The purport of this song is not given. It is called a new song, and was probably similar to the new song of redeeming mercy, of which we hear in chapter v.

After this we have the Song of those who had gotten the victory over the beast, and over his image. 'They sing the song of Moses the servant of God, and the song of the Lamb, saying, Great and marvellous are Thy works, Lord God Almighty; just and true are Thy ways, thou King of saints. Who shall not fear Thee, O Lord, and glorify Thy name? for Thou only art holy: for all nations shall come and worship before Thee; for Thy judgments are made manifest' (Rev. xv. 3, 4).

This seems to have been sung by the ransomed ones exclusively. They are said to have sung the song of Moses and the Lamb,—a song of deliverance, like that of Moses on the shore of the Red Sea,—of deliverance, too, by the blood of the Lamb. This song refers to the righteous judgments of God upon His enemies, and to the result of His judgments in promoting His fear. 'Who shall not fear Thee, O Lord, now that Thy righteous judgments are made manifest?'

We have but another of the Songs of Heaven

given us in the Revelation, and that is one of great
interest, — on the fall and ruin of the mystical
Babylon. ‘ After these things, I heard a great
voice of much people in heaven, saying, Alleluia ;
Salvation, and glory, and honour, and power, unto
the Lord our God : for true and righteous are His
judgments ; for He hath judged the great whore,
which did corrupt the earth with her fornication,
and hath avenged the blood of His servants at her
hand. And again they said, Alleluia. And her
smoke rose up for ever and ever ’ (Rev. xix. 1–3).

In this song, as in others, the retributive justice
of God is celebrated. Heavenly beings praise God
in view of the smoke of the lost, not from motives
of malice and revenge, but from a solemn regard
for the honour of God, the claims of His justice,
and the highest good of the universe ; just as we
rejoice when the murderer is caught, confined, and
brought to suffer the reward of his deeds. We
have no malice against the poor convict. We pity
him, and pray for him. But we rejoice that the
law he has broken is honoured, that justice is vindi-
cated, and that the community is safe.

Judging from the Songs we have examined, heavenly beings think more of the *justice* of God, than
do even good people in the present world. They
praise it more earnestly, and in tender strains.
They speak one to another of the bottomless pit,

and the lake of fire, without any fear of disturbing weak sensibilities, or giving offence.

There is another Song in immediate connection with this—if it be another—in a different strain: ' A voice came out of the throne,'—undoubtedly, from the Messiah—' saying, Praise our God, all ye His servants, and ye that fear Him, both small and great. And I heard as it were the voice of a great multitude, and as the voice of many waters, and as the voice of mighty thunderings, saying, Alleluia: for the Lord God omnipotent reigneth. Let us be glad and rejoice, and give honour to Him : for the marriage of the Lamb is come, and his wife hath made herself ready. And to her was granted that she should be arrayed in fine linen, clean and white: for the fine linen is the righteousness of saints ' (Rev. xix. 5–8).

The last conflict is now nearly over; the millennial marriage of the Lamb is approacing; the bride, the Church, hath received her robe of righteousness, clean and white; she hath made herself ready; and this is sufficient to call forth exultant praises from the hosts of heaven.

From the notices we have taken of the Songs of Heaven, we learn that praise is perhaps the noblest of all employments. It is emphatically the employment of heaven. We hear little or nothing of prayers in heaven, but the whole atmosphere is full of praise. There are in that world not only *stated* ascriptions, like those of the cherubim in Rev. iv. 8, but frequent outbursts of *occasional* worship, in view of great deliverances and triumphs. Such are most of the songs which we find recorded, and on which we have had occasion to remark.

And in these there is an important lesson for us. We, too, have our deliverances, as well as trials; and they should all of them be swift occasions of thanksgiving and praise. Especially should we be exultant in the prosperity of Zion. This is that which calls forth the loudest praises of heaven; and in these praises all those on the earth who have the spirit of heaven will most cordially unite. They will join in these blessed employments here, as they hope to partake of them, with joy unspeak-able and full of glory, in that blessed world for ever.

CHAPTER XXI.

THE LESSONS OF THE APOCALYPSE.

IT would be unpardonable to close this review of the Apocalypse without adverting to some of the important lessons which the book suggests.

1. A thought which strikes us upon the first opening of the book, and which follows us through all its contents, is, *the deep concern which heavenly beings feel in all that pertains to the present world.* They know what is doing here, and what is about to be done, and their active concern in it is unceasing. Angels pour out the vials of God's wrath upon the wicked, and are the unwearied ministers of mercy to His people. While they adore the justice of God in His terrible inflictions, not a victory is gained over the dragon or the beast, but it is celebrated in their triumphal songs. In the study of this wonderful book, we seem to be almost in heaven,—to be mingling in the society of heavenly beings, catching their voices, and partaking of their joys.

The secret of that interest which heavenly beings feel for us on the earth lies, obviously, in *redemption*. It was here that the great Son of God came down, and made an atonement for sin.   It is here that the work of redemption is going forward, and *will* go forward, till the last stone of the heavenly temple is in its place.   The Lamb is the great object of attraction in heaven.   Redemption is God's greatest work—that which best reveals His character, and shows forth His praise.   His brightest glory shines in the face of Jesus Christ.   And since earth is the theatre of redemption—the place of Christ's greatest, mightiest achievements, no wonder that heavenly beings are interested in what is transpiring here. No wonder the seraphim sing above: 'Holy, holy, holy is the Lord God of hosts!   The whole *earth* is full of His glory.'

2. In the Apocalypse we behold, perhaps more clearly than anywhere else, '*both the goodness· and the severity of God.*' This goodness, not only to the ransomed ones who surround His throne and share His glory, but even to those who are ulti- mately cast away from His presence.

Take, for example, Imperial Rome — that beast which Daniel saw,—how long did God's patience endure with this monster, while he was devouring and breaking in pieces, and stamping the residue with his feet?   It was this Roman beast which crucified the Lord, and which tortured and destroyed His people with every form of misery and death, for the next three hundred years. Yet the goodness of God was not to be insulted for ever. Rome's retribution came at length; and it was a frightful one. Read the opening seals, and the first six trumpets, and behold in them the severity of God towards this old and hardened offender. There is 'hail and fire, mingled with blood,' cast upon the Roman earth; there is 'a great mountain burning with fire' dashed into the Roman sea; there is the plague of the locusts let loose from the bottomless pit, to torment the wicked of the earth, till 'men shall seek death and not find it, and desire to die, but death shall flee from them.' There are the 'two hundred thousand thousand' Turkish horsemen, with their breast-plates of iron, with the heads of lions, and fire and brimstone issuing from their mouths, before whom the last remains of the old Roman empire fall to rise no more.

And the same example of goodness and severity is exhibited in God's treatment of Papal Rome. She is permitted to persecute the mystical woman and her seed, and slaughter the faithful witnesses, and blaspheme the name of God and His tabernacle, and make herself drunk with the blood of saints and martyrs, for the long period of twelve hundred and sixty years, until the very souls under the heavenly altar begin to cry out, 'How long, O Lord, holy and true, dost thou not judge and avenge our blood on them that dwell on the earth?' and yet God's patience waits, and His wrath delays. But it does not wait always. A final conflict is provoked, the sword of vengeance falls, and then the severity of God is manifest. Great Babylon falls with a crash that astonishes the nations; a lake of blood issues from the wine-press of God's wrath, by the space of one thousand six hundred furlongs. All the fowls of heaven are summoned together unto the supper of the great God, that they 'may eat the flesh of kings, and the flesh of captains, and the flesh of mighty men, and the flesh of horses, and of them that sit on them, and the flesh of all that follow them, both free and bond, both small and great.' Such is the exhibition here made of God's righteous severity; and all this in the present life. What then must the impression be, as we follow the beast, and the false prophet, and all those who bear their mark, or worship their image, into the lake of fire, and see the smoke of their torment ascending up for ever and ever?

3. While we hear the denunciations of the Apocalypse upon Papal Rome as an organization, and unite with the hosts of heaven in their approval, *we should feel none but the tenderest compassion towards the deluded devotees of this corrupt Church, and*

2 F

should seek, by every proper method, their deliverance and salvation.

Thus God feels towards them. This is evident from His long suffering, His patient forbearance with them. It is further evident in His faithful warnings and admonitions: 'If any man worship the beast and his image, and receive his mark in his forehead, and in his hand, the same shall drink of the wine of the wrath of God, which is poured out without mixture into the cup of His indignation.' 'Come out of her, my people, that ye be not partakers of her sins, and receive not of her plagues.' The distinction here indicated between a system, an organization, and its individual abettors, is a very important one. We may abhor a system, while we pity and pray for those who are involved in it and seduced by it. We may denounce the Romish Church as a ruinous and blasphemous usurpation, and yet do all in our power to enlighten its blinded votaries, and rescue them from its corruptions and its doom.

4. We learn from the Apocalypse, that *whatsoever shall oppose itself to God and His Church must ultimately fall.* So says the prophet Isaiah: 'The nation and kingdom that will not serve Thee shall perish; yea, those nations shall be utterly wasted' (Isa. lx. 11).

We learn the same lesson from what God has

done in other ages. Where now are the kingdoms of Assyria and Egypt,—the oldest of which we have any knowledge? Where is great Nineveh, and the still greater Babylon, which once frowned defiance on all who approached them, and seemed as though they must stand for ever. Where is the Medo-Persian ram which David saw, pushing westward and northward and southward, so that no beast could stand before him, neither could any deliver out of his hand? And where is that Grecian he-goat, which came so rapidly from the west, that he seemed scarcely to touch the ground,—which smote the ram, and brake his two horns, and trampled his empire in the dust? And where is that fourth beast which Daniel saw, dreadful, and terrible, and strong exceedingly, which devoured and brake in pieces with its iron teeth, and stamped the residue with its feet? These mighty empires have long since departed; their cities are in ruins; their names and their history are all that remain to us.

And why have they passed away? Why have they been so utterly and miserably destroyed? With the Bible in our hands, we cannot hesitate for an answer. They set themselves in opposition to the kingdom of Christ, and they could not prosper. They set themselves in the way of the stone cut out of the mountain without hands, and it rolled over them, and ground them to powder.

And so shall it be with every other kingdom which presumes to follow their example. We have in the Apocalypse visions of the future, which are as instructive on this point as events already past. We have here brought before us the last fearful enemies of God and His Church,—the beast, and the false prophet, and the mystical Babylon, drunk with the blood of martyrs and saints. And what is to become of them? What is their end? The beast and the false prophet are taken, and 'cast alive into the lake of fire.' A mighty angel takes up a stone, like a great millstone, and casts it into the sea, saying, 'Thus with violence shall that great city Babylon be thrown down, and shall be found no more at all.'

Let the nations of the earth learn a lesson from these predictions and examples. As true as that there is a God in heaven, He will take care of His people; He will watch over His Church; and whatever opposes itself to the onward progress of this Church and kingdom must inevitably fall.

5. A correct interpretation of the Apocalypse is of great importance, since *it awakens hope, and excites to effort for the advancement of Christ's kingdom.*

Interpretations have, in some instances, been given, which are of an opposite tendency. Some Adventists tell us that the world is growing worse and worse; that nothing can be done to re-

form it till Christ makes His appearance per-
sonally; and that we may as well desist from all
further efforts to advance His kingdom. But such
is not the tendency of the views which we have
presented. We have seen that there is to be a
millennium,—a long period of rest and peace to the
Church, and that this happy day is near at hand.
The symbolic seals have all been opened; the first
six trumpets have been sounded; the first five vials
have been poured out; the twelve hundred and
sixty years are drawing to a close; and every thing
on the prophetic page is indicating that the latter
day glory of the Church is near.

Meanwhile, the providence of God is teaching
the same lesson. The Bible is translated into all
languages, and circulated in all lands; the Gospel
is preached in thousands of places where, until
recently, it has not been named; doors long shut
against the truth are now opened, and obstructions
hitherto insurmountable are taken out of the way.
The Pope is shorn of his temporal dominions, and
is becoming weak as any other man. In short,
the signs of the times, like the prophetic symbols,
are unitedly indicating that millennial scenes are
near at hand.

Now all these things should operate—we trust
they are operating—as incitements to increased
exertion in this holy cause.

In the great work of preparation for the coming glory, our Divine Master has assigned to each Christian his place, and He expects that every one will do his duty. There must be no indolence or desertion in so good a cause; no sleeping on the watch; no faintness of heart or feebleness of hands; no parleying, dallying, or compromising with the enemy. Every friend of Christ must now be a fast friend, a liberal friend, a devoted and unfailing friend. Every friend of Christ must possess, in large measure, the Spirit of Christ, and suffer no contradiction of sinners to deprive him of this. With meekness and kindness, with humility and gentleness, weak in ourselves, but *strong in the Lord*, we must go forth together to the work assigned us, prepared to meet dangers, to make sacrifices, and (if it must be so) to suffer death, in the service of Him who laid down His life for us.

The scriptural views of the millennium inculcated by such men as Bellamy, Hopkins, Fuller, and many others, near the beginning of the present century, contributed not a little to arouse the Christian world to effort for the universal spread of the Gospel, and led on to that new state of things, and to those bright and animating prospects which we now behold. And the same views, we trust, will continue to operate, and with increased force, until the whole world is given to Christ; and His spiritual reign shall be universal.

6. I remark, finally, that the Apocalypse, rightly interpreted, is calculated *to afford encouragement and comfort to the people of God, even in the darkest times.*

This was the original design of the book; and this design it has answered all along through the ages, and will continue to answer, till the end comes. In the early days of Pagan persecution, and in the later Papal persecutions, we can hardly conceive how much consolation the poor distressed Christians have taken in reading and pondering this blessed book. In their lonely prisons, in their secluded haunts, in the dungeons of the Inquisition and the Bastile, in dens and caves of the earth, with this book in their hands or in their memories, they could see light ahead. They could see their covenant God and Redeemer 'riding on the whirlwind and directing the storm,' causing the wrath of man to praise Him; over-ruling all things for the good of His people, and sure to end the fearful conflict in glorious victory and abiding peace.

And Christians, under all circumstances, are entitled to partake of the same consolations. This fountain of love is ever open, and its resources are exhaustless. Draw near, then, afflicted believer —whether in sickness or bereavements, in worldly

disappointments or spiritual wants—come and draw
living water from these wells of salvation. Come
and see the glorious termination of all your conflicts, and the conflicts of God's people upon earth,
and unite your voices with those in heaven, saying, *Alleluia, for the Lord God omnipotent reigneth.*

APPENDIX.

———◆———

THE description of Ezekiel's City and Temple is contained in the last eight chapters of his prophecy. This portion of the inspired word, it is presumed, is very little read, and that because it cannot be understood. Christians are in doubt respecting it; they know not what to make of it, and so pass it by.

The description before us is prefaced by the resurrection in the valley of dry bones, denoting the conversion of Israel in the latter days, and their seeming restoration to their own land (Ezek. xxxvii.). This is followed by a tremendous assault upon them by Gog and Magog, and other enemies, in which converted Israel, or, in other words, the Church of God, is delivered.

This is very like the great conflict immediately preceding the millennium, of which we hear so much in the Revelation. Indeed, some of the phraseology is strikingly similar to that in the Revelation, and may have suggested to John a portion of his imagery. For example, in the nine-

teenth chapter of the Revelation, all the fowls of
heaven are summoned together unto the supper
of the great God, that they 'may eat the flesh
of kings, and the flesh of captains, and the flesh
of mighty men, and the flesh of horses, and of
them that sit on them, and the flesh of all men,
both free and bond, both small and great' (Rev.
xix. 18). So also in Ezekiel: 'Thus saith the
Lord God; Speak unto every feathered fowl, and
to every beast of the field, Assemble yourselves,
and come; gather yourselves on every side to my
sacrifice that I do sacrifice for you, even a great
sacrifice upon the mountains of Israel, that ye may
eat flesh, and drink blood. Ye shall eat the flesh
of the mighty, and drink the blood of the princes
of the earth, of rams, of lambs, and of goats, of
bullocks, all of them fatlings of Bashan. And ye
shall eat fat till ye be full, and drink blood till ye be
drunken, of my sacrifice which I have sacrificed for
you. Thus ye shall be filled at my table with horses
and chariots, with mighty men, and with all men of
war, saith the Lord God' (Ezek. xxxix. 17–20).

Immediately following this is Ezekiel's vision
of the temple to be built, running out into a minute
particularity, and extending through the three following chapters.

The temple being prepared, the God of Israel
returns to take up His abode in it. 'The glory of

the Lord came into the house by the way of the gate whose prospect is toward the east. So the spirit took me up, and brought me into the inner court; and, behold, the glory of the Lord filled the house' (Ezek. xliii. 4, 5).

Next the altar is measured, and its ordinances of worship are described. The services of the priests and Levites also are appointed (Ezek. xliv.).

The Land of Promise, as described by Ezekiel, is very different from that in which Israel had before dwelt. It is in shape a quadrangle or parallelogram, about a hundred miles in length from north to south, and fifty in breadth from east to west. Nearly half of the central portion of it, where stand the city and the temple, is reserved for the priests and Levites, and for other public uses. The remaining portions of it, on the northern and southern extremities, are set apart, severally, for the twelve tribes of Israel, each tribe having a narrow strip running entirely across the territory from east to west.

From the foundation of the temple, on the east side, Ezekiel saw water issuing forth in small quantity. But as he traced it, the stream constantly increased, until it became a river which he could not cross. It ran along in a south-easterly direction—its banks being crowned with fruitful trees—until it emptied its waters into the Dead

Sea, which (strange to tell) was at once cleansed from its nauseous, deadly qualities, and became fruitful in all kinds of fish. The imagery here, as in the city which John describes in the last two chapters of the Revelation, is borrowed from the terrestrial paradise—the garden of Eden. In each of the three there is a river, the banks of which are crowned with life-giving, health-restoring, trees. The city of Ezekiel is also, in some respects, like that of John. It lay four square, having three gates on each side—twelve in all—which bore the names of the twelve tribes of Israel; it was a splendid city, and it had a glorious name—Jehovah Shammah—the Lord is there.

Without going further into a description of the renovated Palestine, the city and temple of Ezekiel, let us pause and inquire, What do these things mean? What is their import and interpretation?

One thing is certain, these predictions of Ezekiel have not yet been fulfilled. The twelve tribes of Israel have not been converted and restored to their own land. This land has not been divided in the manner set forth by the prophet; nor has such a city and temple as he describes been built. Jerusalem and the temple were rebuilt after the return of a portion of the Jews from Babylon, but not in the style foretold by Ezekiel, nor anything approaching it.

Another question arises : Will these predictions ever have a literal fulfilment ? Was such the intention of the Spirit who indited them ? The descriptions throughout look like a literal fulfilment. They are so minute and particular, as almost to force upon one the idea of such a fulfilment. But will it ever be realised ? It must be borne in mind, that if we insist upon a literal fulfilment, we must carry it honestly through. If any part of the prediction is to be taken literally, all must be. The question returns then : Are we to suppose that this prediction of Ezekiel ever will be literally fulfilled ?

I think not. The supposition is inadmissible, if not impossible. It can never be. Who believes that the Holy Land, now somewhat irregularly shaped, is ever to be transformed into a quadrangle such as has been described ; and that the twelve tribes of Israel—each a distinct community—are to be recovered and settled there ? Or, if they should be, who believes that they would be willing to give up nearly half of their small territory to the priests and Levites, and other officials, reserving to themselves only twelve narrow strips, running across the country from east to west ? Nor is this the worst of it : How long could the twelve tribes of Israel live on these narrow strips, embracing at the farthest not more than three thousand square miles—a tenth part as much as the state of Maine? Who can believe that a temple, such as Ezekiel describes, is yet to be built in Palestine, and that the entire Mosaic ritual, with its feasts and fasts, its bloody sacrifices and offerings, is to be established there, and that too for *converted Christian men*, when the apostles assure us that Judaism, as such, is dead, and that the ritual of Moses has vanished away? Who believes that a stream of water, small at first, but miraculously increased as it passes along, until it becomes a mighty river, is to issue from the foundations of this new temple, and pour its waters into the Dead Sea, removing at once the nauseous deadly qualities of the sea, and filling it with fish and other living creatures. If Ezekiel's vision is to be accepted literally, then all these things are to come to pass; and yet who believes them? Who can believe them?

The question returns then, What is the import of Ezekiel's vision, and of the chapters on which we have remarked? How are they to be understood? And what were they designed to teach? We answer: They are to be understood, not literally, but, like the Apocalypse, symbolically; and thus interpreted, they are full of rich and glorious meaning. Thus the resurrection of the dry bones is a symbol, teaching the future conversion of the Jews, and perhaps of the Gentiles also, to Christ. The assault of Gog and Magog portends the great conflict which is to usher in the millennium. The city with its surroundings, and the temple with its services, set forth the glory of the millennial Church, and the purity of its worship. The stream issuing from the temple, and pouring into the Dead Sea to heal its waters and fill it with life, is a beautiful symbol of the healing influences of the sanctuary of God. If this world of death is ever to be recovered to Christ, it must be by an influence such as this. Such, as it seems to me, are some of the teachings of Ezekiel's vision,—more rich and glorious infinitely, than any literal interpretation can be.

And if it be inquired further, why the symbolical method of teaching was here adopted—why, if the Divine Spirit wished to inculcate lessons such as these, He did not do it in plain, literal, didactic terms? I have only to answer, that Ezekiel was a Jew and a priest, and those to be instructed and comforted by him were Jews. All their ideas of religion were associated with a *temple service*—with the official work of the priests, and the sacrifices and offerings of the temple. Hence, the promise of great spiritual blessings—a great and future revival of religion—must be made to them in connection with a new city and temple. It could be made intelligibly in no other way. The pious in Israel were encouraged and comforted by the vision of Ezekiel, as they could not have been if the prediction had been given in more literal terms.

It is for us, who have the brighter light and more spiritual teachings of the Gospel, to look through the shadows to the substance—to study these venerable symbols, and gather from them the rich and glorious instructions which they were intended to impart.

THE END.

www.ingramcontent.com/pod-product-compliance
Lightning Source LLC
Chambersburg PA
CBHW030805020726
47499CB00006B/1777